NATIONAL AUDUBON SOCIETY

FIRST FIELD GUIDE

MAMMALS

NATIONAL AUDUBON SOCIETY

FIRST FIELD GUIDE

MAMMALS

Written by

John Grassy and Chuck Keene

Scholastic Inc.

New York   Toronto   London   Auckland   Sydney

The National Audubon Society, established in 1905, has 550,000 members and more than 500 chapters nationwide. Its mission is to conserve and restore natural ecosystems, focusing on birds and other wildlife, and these guides are part of that mission. Celebrating the beauty and wonders of nature, Audubon looks toward its second century of educating people of all ages. For information about Audubon membership, contact:

National Audubon Society

700 Broadway

New York, NY 10003-9562

212-979-3000   800-274-4201

http://www.audubon.org

Copyright © 1998 by Chanticleer Press, Inc.
All rights reserved. Published by Scholastic Inc.
SCHOLASTIC and associated logos are trademarks and/or registered trademarks of Scholastic Inc.

LIBRARY OF CONGRESS CATALOGING-IN-PUBLICATION DATA
Grassy, John.
  National Audubon Society first field guide. Mammals.
    p.   cm.
  Includes index.
  Summary: Explores the world of mammals, identifying their characteristics and describing individual species.
    ISBN 0-590-05471-6 (hc). — ISBN 0-590-05489-9 (pb)
    1. Mammals—Juvenile literature.   2. Mammals—Identification —Juvenile literature.   [1. Mammals.]   I. Keene, Chuck I. II. National Audubon Society.   III. Title.
QL706.2.G73   1998
599—dc21   98-2939

ISBN 0-590-05471-6 (HC)
ISBN 0-590-05489-9 (PB)

10 9 8 7 6 5 4 3 2 1   8   9/9   0/0   01   02 03

Printed in Hong Kong
First printing, September 1998

Contents

About this book

American Marten page 109

Whether you are watching mammals in your own backyard, walking in a park, or hiking in the mountains, this book will help you look at mammals the way a naturalist does. The book is divided into four parts:

PART 1: The world of mammals gives you lots of interesting information about mammals and how they live, such as what they eat, how they raise their young, and how they survive in the wild.

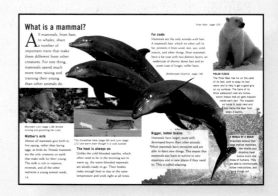

What is a mammal?

All mammals, from bats to whales, share a number of important traits that make them different from other creatures. For one thing, mammals spend much more time raising and training their young than other animals do.

Mountain Lion (page 118) female nursing and grooming her cubs

Mother's milk
Almost all mammals give birth to live young, rather than laying eggs, as birds do. Female mammals are the only creatures on earth that make milk for their young. The milk is rich in vitamins, minerals, and all the other nutrients a young animal needs.

This Snowshoe Hare (page 66) and Lynx (page 121) are warm even though it is cold outside

The heat is always on
Unlike the cold-blooded reptiles, which often need to lie in the morning sun to warm up, the warm-blooded mammals are always ready to go. Their bodies make enough heat to stay at the same temperature and work right at all times.

Fur coats
Mammals are the only animals with hair. A mammal's hair, which we often call its fur, protects it from wind, rain, sun, cold, insects, and other things. Most mammals have a fur coat with two distinct layers: an undercoat of shorter dense hair and an outer coat of longer, stiffer hairs.

Bottlenose Dolphins page 148

Polar Bear page 120

POLAR FLEECE
The Polar Bear has fur on the pads of its feet, both to keep its feet warm and to help it get a good grip on icy surfaces. The hairs of its thick waterproof coat are hollow, which means that air gets trapped inside each hair. The trapped air holds in body heat and also helps the Bear float when it swims.

Bigger, better brains
Mammals have larger, more well-developed brains than other animals. Most mammals can learn to do new things. This means that mammals can learn to survive in new situations and in new places if they need to. This is called adapting.

A WHALE OF A BRAIN
Scientists believe that large marine mammals, like whales and dolphins have brains much like those of humans. They are able to communicate, follow instructions, and figure things out.

Putting it all together

The field guide will help you to identify the mammals that you see. But how do you tell a Coyote from a Gray Wolf or a Mule Deer from a White-tailed Deer? The clues below will help you learn what sort of details to look for.

Shape
Mammals often have a distinctive shape or profile. Some small mammals may look similar, but their shapes can help you identify them. For example, mice have rounded bodies, long tails, and big ears, while shrews have longer bodies, long, pointed noses, no visible ears, and short tails.

The Grizzly Bear (page 105) has a big hump above its shoulders, the Black Bear (page 104) does not.

The Black Bear's face looks straight and cone-shaped in profile, but the Grizzly's face curves inward slightly and is wider.

Color and markings
Even species that look alike have differences, often in their color and markings. It is easy to confuse ground squirrels with chipmunks in some western states. The best way to tell them apart is by markings: chipmunks have facial stripes; ground squirrels do not.

Least Chipmunk page 71

Golden-mantled Ground Squirrel page 75

Mule Deer (page 125) antlers have two main branches on each side.

The antlers of the White-tailed Deer (page 124) feature one main horizontal branch on each side, with smaller branches growing upward.

The Elk's (page 126) very large antlers have short branches growing forward over the face and larger ones growing over the back.

Special features
Horns and antlers look similar but are not the same. Horns, which grow on members of the cattle family, like Mountain Goats and Bighorn Sheep, remain on the head year-round. Antlers, worn by deer, are grown new each year and shed after the mating season.

Red Fox page 102

Size
Size can help you identify animals that look similar. Beavers and muskrats may live in the same lake, but you will not mistake one for the other when you learn that a beaver weighs up to 60 pounds, while the largest muskrat weighs no more than 4 pounds.

How can you tell foxes, Coyotes, and wolves apart? Check out the size. A Red Fox weighs about 8 to 15 pounds, a Coyote weighs 20 to 40, and a Gray Wolf weighs up to 130 pounds.

Coyote page 98

Gray Wolf page 100

PART 2: How to look at mammals tells you where mammals live, how to find clues that tell you mammals are in an area, how to look at tracks, and how to identify the mammals that you do see.

PART 3: The field guide gives detailed descriptions, range maps, track drawings, and dramatic photographs of 50 common North American mammals. There are also photographs and short descriptions of 79 look-alike species that you might see.

PART 4: The reference section at the back of the book includes a helpful glossary of terms used by mammalogists; lists of useful books, videos, CDs, Web sites, and organizations; a metric conversion chart; and an index of species covered in the field guide.

What is a naturalist?

A naturalist is a person who studies nature. Some naturalists are scientists (mammalogists are scientists who study mammals), but others are ordinary people. You can be a naturalist, too, even in your yard or at the park. Begin by watching, listening, and asking questions. If you watch the squirrels in your yard over the course of a year, you will learn a lot about them and their environment.

L. David Mech

STUDIES WITH WOLVES

L. David Mech (pronounced MEECH) is a mammalogist who studies wolves. He has spent time in the wild in Alaska and Canada watching how wolves live, how they behave in their family groups, and what animals they hunt. He has also been a friend to the wolves by working to bring them back to places where they no longer live, such as Yellowstone National Park.

LEWIS AND CLARK: DARING EXPLORERS, SELF-TAUGHT NATURALISTS

Meriwether Lewis and William Clark explored the West long before it was settled by pioneers. During their two-year expedition (1804–1806), they kept detailed journals describing wildlife that had never been written about before, like prairie dogs.

Lewis and Clark (in uniforms) at the Missouri River

Essential equipment

When you go mammal-watching, bring a pair of binoculars so you can get "close-ups" of animals without disturbing them. Bring a pad and pencils for notes or sketches. And take your field guide so you can identify what you see.

Rules for mammal-watching

- Take a partner with you, preferably an adult.
- Leave pets at home. Dogs can scare away or harm the mammals you want to see.
- Never approach or touch any wild animal. Young mammals that appear abandoned usually have parents that will rush out to protect them and very possibly harm you. If you think an animal is sick or hurt, contact your state wildlife agency.
- Do not feed animals. It is not good for them, and in national parks and wildlife refuges it is against the law.
- Do not disturb animals. Good observers are quiet and careful.
- Stay on trails. Do not trample plants, break branches, or otherwise change the area you are exploring. Just about everything in that area is important to the animals that live in it.

The world of mammals

There are about 4,000 kinds of mammals in the world, and more than 400 of them live in North America. Their ability to live in many places and in many ways is amazing. You can find mammals on land, at sea, in the air, and under the ground.

Land-roving

Far-roaming wolves, fast-running deer, mountain-climbing goats, and tree-dwelling chipmunks are just some of the many types of mammals that live on land. These mammals may not look alike—but they are all suited to the life they lead on land.

Mountain Goat
page 134

Airborne

Bats are the only mammals in the world that can fly under their own power. Their wings are made of skin that is stretched along their arms and between their fingers. Flying squirrels leap and glide through the air but don't have wings to flap.

Eastern Red Bat

Underground

There's a world of mammals beneath your feet. Ground squirrels and mice dig elaborate burrows with separate areas for eating, sleeping, and raising young. Moles tunnel through the ground in search of prey. During the cold mountain winters, pikas stay warm in their tunnels and dens.

American Pika (page 62) at entrance to den

Seafaring

Whales and dolphins may look like fish and act like fish, but they are mammals. They swim and dive underwater but must return to the surface for air.

Seals, sea lions, and walruses find food and shelter in the ocean but come ashore to rest, breed, and give birth.

Common Dolphin page 149

The animal kingdom

Scientists separate animals into groups. The largest group is the animal kingdom. Every animal in the world belongs to it. Next, each animal is placed in a group called a phylum. Each phylum is separated into classes, each class into orders, and each order into families. Every family is divided into genera (plural of genus), which are subdivided into species.

THE NAME GAME

Why don't scientists use everyday, or common, names instead of Latin ones? Because the same animal may have more than one common name. In some parts of the United States, for example, people call Coyotes "Prairie Wolves." This is confusing because it sounds like there are two different animals instead of just one. There is no confusion at all, however, when just one scientific name is used. What is the Coyote's scientific name? *Canis latrans*.

Kingdom: Animalia
Phylum: Chordata
Class: Mammalia
Order: Carnivora
Family: Canidae
Genus: *Mustela*
Species: *nivalis*
(Least Weasel)

Kingdom: Animalia
Phylum: Chordata
Class: Mammalia
Order: Rodentia
Family: Sciuridae
Genus: *Tamias*
Species: *striatus*
(Eastern Chipmunk)

TWO MAMMALS CLASSIFIED

Notice that the Least Weasel and the Eastern Chipmunk both belong to the same phylum, Chordata, and the same class, Mammalia. There the similarity ends. The two mammals belong to different orders, families, genera, and species.

WHAT'S IN A NAME?

Each mammal has a scientific name that is used around the world. The scientific name for the White-tailed Deer is *Odocoileus virginianus.* The first part of the name, *Odocoileus,* is the genus name, which is shared with close relatives. The second part is the species name, which is given only to that animal.

White-tailed Deer page 124

Coyote page 98

What is a species?

When we talk about a kind of mammal, like a Coyote or a Wolverine, we are usually talking about a species. The members of a species look alike and can breed with one another. They usually cannot breed with other species. The Gray Wolf and the Red Wolf are two species of wolves. They look different and cannot breed with each other.

What is a mammal?

All mammals, from bats to whales, share a number of important traits that make them different from other creatures. For one thing, mammals spend much more time raising and training their young than other animals do.

Mountain Lion (page 118) female nursing and grooming her cubs

Mother's milk

Almost all mammals give birth to live young, rather than laying eggs, as birds do. Female mammals are the only creatures on earth that make milk for their young. The milk is rich in vitamins, minerals, and all the other nutrients a young animal needs.

This Snowshoe Hare (page 66) and Lynx (page 121) are warm even though it is cold outside

The heat is always on

Unlike the cold-blooded reptiles, which often need to lie in the morning sun to warm up, the warm-blooded mammals are always ready to go. Their bodies make enough heat to stay at the same temperature and work right at all times.

Polar Bear page 105

Fur coats

Mammals are the only animals with hair. A mammal's hair, which we often call its fur, protects it from wind, rain, sun, cold, insects, and other things. Most mammals have a fur coat with two distinct layers: an undercoat of shorter dense hair and an outer coat of longer, stiffer hairs.

Bottlenosed Dolphins page 148

POLAR FLEECE

The Polar Bear has fur on the pads of its feet, both to keep its feet warm and to help it get a good grip on icy surfaces. The hairs of its thick waterproof coat are hollow, which means that air gets trapped inside each hair. The trapped air holds in body heat and also helps the bear float when it swims.

Bigger, better brains

Mammals have larger, more well-developed brains than other animals. Most mammals have memories and are able to learn new things. This means that mammals can learn to survive in new situations and in new places if they need to. This is called adapting.

A WHALE OF A BRAIN

Scientists believe that large marine mammals like whales and dolphins have brains much like those of humans. They are able to communicate, follow instructions, and figure things out.

15

Mammal bodies

M ost mammals have four legs and a tail, but not all do. Humans, for instance, have two legs but no tail. Whales have a tail but no legs. No matter what a mammal's body looks like, you can bet that it is specially adapted for the kind of life that animal leads.

UNDERGROUND SWIMMERS

Mammals like pocket gophers and moles that spend most of their time underground usually have strong claws and forelimbs. The mole's forelimbs are turned so that the palms face backward and the elbows point upward. With strong chest muscles attached to the forelimbs, the mole seems to "swim" through the soil, like a person doing the breaststroke.

Star-nosed Mole   page 55

FINS, FLIPPERS, FLUKES

The bodies of marine mammals are long and bulletlike, a good shape for swimming. Whales and dolphins move using powerful up-and-down thrusts of their tails, which are divided into two identical sections called flukes. Their front flippers and the fin along the back provide steering and keep them upright. Seals sweep their hind limbs back and forth and steer with their front flippers. Sea lions move forward using their front flippers; their hind limbs are used for steering.

California Sea Lion page 140

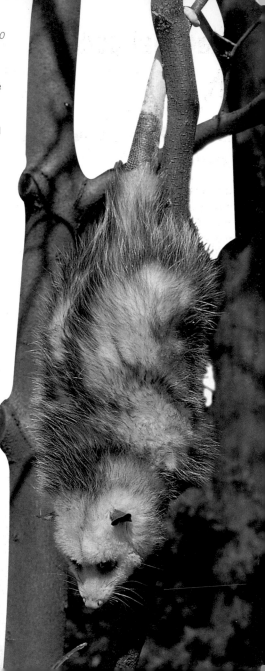

Virginia Opossum page 50

TAIL TOOLS

Tails provide steering, balance, even protection from weather. Some antelope squirrels use their tails as portable shade in the desert. Beaver tails act as rudders in the water, to help the animal steer. A fox's tail provides balance as the fox leaps and runs. The opossum has a prehensile (grasping) tail that acts like an extra hand, wrapping around branches so the animal can hang from tree limbs.

Pronghorn page 130

HOOVES AND CLAWS

Some of the fastest runners in the world are long-legged mammals, such as the Pronghorn, Moose, Elk, and White-tailed Deer. These animals have long foot bones and they run on the tips of their toes. The toes are protected by hooves, which are made from a tough substance called keratin. Mammal claws are also made of keratin, but claws do not help mammals run. They help them climb, dig, and grasp and hold prey. Wildcats have claws that can be pulled in when they are not in use.

Mammal senses

Sight, hearing, smell, and touch help mammals do two important things: locate food and avoid danger.

Mule Deer
page 125

Hearing

Most mammals can hear sounds too high or far away for people to hear. Large ears that swivel in all directions, like those of the Mule Deer, are better at gathering sounds. How much better? Cup your hand around one ear and listen—you can easily hear the difference.

REFLECTIONS

The eyes of some night-active mammals, like this Bobcat (page 120), are made for seeing in the dark. A reflector at the back of the eyes absorbs dim light and reflects it back. This is what makes an animal's eyes appear to glow in the dark when light strikes them.

White-footed Mouse page 83

Sight

What a mammal sees depends on whether it is a predator (hunter) or prey (food for hunters). The eyes of most predators, such as the Bobcat, point forward and are close together so they can quickly focus before leaping or pouncing. The eyes of prey species, such as mice, look to the sides so they can see all around.

18

MAMMAL RADAR

Many kinds of bats use their ears as eyes. They make ultrasonic squeals (which are so high they cannot be heard by humans) while flying in the dark. The sounds bounce off objects like trees or insects and return to the bat's ears. In this way, the bat knows what lies ahead—and can zero in on a tasty mosquito!

Eastern Pipistrelle
page 59

Smell

Smell is all-important for many mammals. Bears have poor vision and hearing and rely on their keen noses to find food. Deer smell the breeze for signs of danger. Territorial mammals, such as Coyotes and wolves, mark their territories with urine to let others know that the area is claimed.

Black Bear page 104

Touch

Some mammals have whiskers that are rooted in bundles of nerves on the face. Sea lions use their whiskers to detect the movements of fish underwater. Moles have extremely poor vision, not a particularly important sense for mammals that live underground. The Star-nosed Mole uses its highly sensitive snout to feel its way through tunnels and locate food.

Northern Sea
Lion page 141

What do mammals eat?

Mammals eat many kinds of foods—plants, meat, fish, insects. Their teeth are designed for what they eat. Sharp pointed teeth are best for tearing flesh, while broad flat teeth are good for grinding up vegetation.

Rodents

Like all rodents, beavers have long razor-sharp front teeth. The upper teeth grip, while the lower ones gnaw. Beavers use both sets to shave the strips of tree bark they like to eat.

American Beaver page 92

Carnivores

Many carnivores (meat eaters), such as lions and wolves, are fast-moving predators that can run down prey. Their long sharp canine teeth are designed for grabbing onto and stabbing other animals. Killer Whales (or Orcas) behave much like land carnivores, chasing and killing seals, fish, and penguins.

The Walrus, a carnivore, rakes the ocean floor with its long tusks, looking for clams to eat.

GIGANTIC APPETITE

Powered by a tiny heart that may beat 1,000 times per minute, shrews eat night and day, taking only brief rest periods. They feed mainly on worms, plants, insects, and grubs.

Northern Short-tailed Shrew (page 52) with prey

MICROSCOPIC DIET

The largest mammals in the world eat the smallest foods. Blue and Humpback Whales feed on tiny plants called plankton. Instead of teeth, their mouths have large brushlike structures called baleen. As water rushes into a whale's mouth, the baleen strains out the plankton.

Humpback Whales (page 144) feeding

Grazers and browsers

Deer, Moose, and Pronghorns eat grasses, leaves, and twigs. They often have to eat in wide-open spaces, like fields, where they feed rapidly on large amounts of food. Then they move into safer areas and bring the meal up from the stomach. This partially eaten mass of food is called the "cud." The animals then chew the cud and finish digesting it in peace.

Moose (page 128) grazing on pond grass

Attack and defend

For a wild animal, surviving each day can be hard. Carnivores use speed, strength, and intelligence to catch a meal. Prey species often have to think fast to protect themselves.

MAKING A GETAWAY

What would you do if you were being chased by a predator? Probably the same thing most wild animals do: run and hide. Prairie dogs dive into their burrows. Squirrels head for safety in trees. The House Mouse rushes for cover—like behind your refrigerator!

Eastern Gray Squirrel page 78

BLENDING IN

Some mammals have coloring that helps them blend in with their environment. This is called camouflage. The Snowshoe Hare is brown in the summer, white in the winter, and brown and white in the spring when the ground is patched with snow.

Snowshoe Hare (page 66)
in its winter coat

Elk page 126

Striped Skunk page 114

KICKOFF TIME!

Male Elk and Moose have huge antlers but do not often use them as weapons. Instead, they use their razor-sharp hooves. Predators like Mountain Lions or wolves are close to the ground and easy to kick.

WHAT A STINK!

When threatened, skunks launch a stream of rancid eye-burning musk. Most of the time a skunk does not even need to use its weaponry. It simply stomps its feet—the signal that it is ready to spray—and the enemy runs away.

A SHARP DEFENSE

The slow, clumsy porcupine is protected by thousands of quills on its tail and back. The quills are extremely sharp and painful—and can even kill.

Common Porcupine page 96

PREDATORS IN ACTION

The Mountain Lion is a superb hunter. It can leap more than 20 feet in a single bound and run faster than a deer for short distances. Mountain Lions creep up close to their prey and then leap onto the victim's back, holding it long enough to deliver a bite on the neck.

Mountain Lion page 118

Mating and having babies

Most North American mammals do not pair up for life. Males and females find each other during mating season and go their separate ways soon after, leaving the females to raise the young.

Who gets to mate?

Male mammals of many species battle to decide who gets to mate. They may use calls, have staring contests, bite, kick, or butt heads. Usually the winner is decided before there are any serious injuries.

Litters and lifespans

Mammals that have only one or two babies at a time usually live for many years. A bat can live for 30 years, a long time for a wild animal. Most bats give birth to just one baby each spring. Animals that do not live very long, like mice and other prey species, breed several times a year and have large litters.

The Meadow Vole has lots of babies—it has to, since it may live for only a year. In their speedy cycle of life and death, female voles start having babies when they are just 8 to 12 weeks old! They have up to 12 litters a year, of 2 to 10 young each time.

24   *Meadow Vole (page 90) babies in nest*

WHY FIGHT IT OUT?

Because the strongest, healthiest male is the best choice for fathering youngsters that will grow up to be strong and healthy, too.

Male Dall's Sheep (page 137) in head-butting contest

SINGING FOR A MATE?

Male Humpback Whales gather in their breeding grounds and "sing," producing a series of chirps, cries, and other sounds. Individuals sing for 10 or 15 minutes at a time, but the entire group may go on much longer. Naturalists aren't completely sure why Humpbacks do this but suspect it is how males tell females they are good partners for mating.

Humpback Whales page 144

The Grizzly Bear can live 15 to 35 years. A female may give birth once every three years, usually to two cubs at a time.

Grizzly Bear cub page 105

DEN BABIES

Many mammals have their babies in dens or burrows.
The den is a safe place, hidden from people and
predators. It might be inside a fallen tree or beneath
a dense tangle of rocks and brush. Weasels build a
soft nest using fur from animals they have killed.
The den may be the abandoned burrow of a
chipmunk or pocket gopher or a hollow spot under a
tree stump. Weasels have four to eight babies in a
litter, all born blind and without hair.

Short-tailed Weasel (page 111) babies in nest

LODGE BABIES

Baby beavers, called kits,
are born inside the family
lodge, a large mound of tree
limbs and mud with a
hidden chamber inside. Kits
are born with their eyes
open and a full coat of hair.
Within a week they are
excellent swimmers.

*American Beaver (page 92)
with kit in lodge*

OCEAN BABIES

Baby dolphins are born in
deep water and must swim to
the surface for their first
breath of air. The mother
dolphin often dives under her
baby to help steer it in the
right direction. Dolphins have
one baby at a time, born
about a year after mating.

26

Bottlenosed Dolphin (page 148) mother and baby

POUCH BABIES

Opossums are born long before they are able to survive on their own. After birth, they crawl up the mother's body and into a pouch on her belly. Each baby latches onto a nipple and remains in the pouch, attached to the mother, for at least two months. The pouch protects the young while they grow.

Virginia Opossum (page 50)
young in mother's pouch

HIDDEN BABIES

Pronghorns have their babies in a hidden spot on the open plains but soon join a herd of other mothers and fawns. Females, called does, have one fawn their first year but in following years have twins or occasionally triplets.

Pronghorn (page 130) mother and fawns

ICE BABIES

Like many seals in the Arctic, the Harp Seal is born on bare ice, where its white fur helps it blend in. It receives milk from its mother for only two weeks, but by that time it already weighs 100 pounds!

Baby Harp Seal on ice

27

Raising the young

Young mammals are not ready to "leave home" until they know how to take care of themselves. They need to know what kind of food to eat and how to get it. They need to know how to avoid danger and how to protect themselves. They need time to learn.

MOM: THE CENTRAL FIGURE

The typical mammal family is a mother and her young. Mom is teacher, protector, and provider of food. At first she nurses her babies with milk; later she leaves to find food and bring it back to them. Raccoons are born in spring and are off mother's milk by late summer. Their mother shows them how to climb a tree quickly to escape predators; how to swim; and how to catch mice, frogs, and crickets.

Common Raccoon (page 106)
mother and babies

MOM ON GUARD

Mothers are extremely protective of their babies and fight to defend them. A mother Black Bear or Moose can be very dangerous—even for people. If she sees another animal in the area, she will charge at it to keep her young safe.

Moose (page 128)
mother and baby

HITCHING A RIDE

Keeping up with mom can be hard at first. So some mammal babies take the easy way out. Young opossums hitch a ride on their mother's back. Baby beavers get a lift on their mother's broad flat tail. Sea Otter babies nap on their mother's chest as she floats in the ocean.

Sea Otter (page 117)
mother carrying pup

MAMMAL DADS

Some male mammals stick around to help with the young. These include Northern River Otters, American Badgers, and Red Foxes. The Coyote, Gray Wolf, and American Beaver form a lifelong bond with one female. They help hunt or gather food once the babies are weaned and they protect them from danger.

Mountain Lions (page 118) challenging each other over territory

BREAKING AWAY

Eventually a mammal must leave its mother's side. Young bats become members of the colony. Deer and sheep continue to live with the herd they grew up in. But getting started alone is more difficult for carnivores. After living with their mother for about 18 months, young Mountain Lions must find a new territory of their own. Older stronger Mountain Lions occupy the best areas and will drive out newcomers. Some young adults may starve or be killed before they find a new home.

29

Social life

Some mammals, like the Woodchuck, are solitary, living alone most of the year and coming together with a partner only to mate. But many others live in groups. The group's members often cooperate to find food, raise their young, and protect themselves.

BODY LANGUAGE

Mammals communicate in many ways. The White-tailed Deer raises its tail to signal danger to other deer. Rabbits and hares thump the ground with a hind leg at the first sign of danger; others feel the vibrations through the pads on their feet.

Desert Cottontail (page 65) thumping its hind leg

ON THE TOWN

Hundreds, sometimes thousands, of Black-tailed Prairie Dogs live in underground "towns." Each town is divided into neighborhoods made up of different family groups. Prairie dogs work together to build tunnels and burrows. They also take turns standing guard, using special calls to warn town members of danger or to signal that all is clear. Prairie dogs often touch noses, a friendly greeting for a relative or neighbor.

Black-tailed Prairie Dog page 76

Mule Deer (page 125) bucks with summer antlers

BOYS' CLUB

At certain times of year, some male mammals leave their herd or colony and form bachelor groups. Mule Deer bucks spend the spring and summer grazing and traveling in small bands of three or more. The deer in each band are of similar age or size. As fall approaches, bachelor groups rejoin their herds for the mating season.

LIFE IN THE PACK

Gray Wolves form packs of four to seven wolves that are usually related. The largest strongest male is the pack leader. He is called the "alpha male." If any pack member needs to be reminded of who is in charge, the alpha male wolf shows its fangs or raises the hair along its back and neck.

CALL OF THE WILD

Wolves howl to let other wolves know where they are. Sometimes the whole pack howls together, usually before going on a hunt.

Gray Wolf (page 100) howling

Alpha male Gray Wolf showing pack member who is boss

Hibernation and migration

Surviving the winter can be difficult. Keeping warm and finding food in freezing weather take lots of energy. Some mammals survive by hibernating, or going into a long sleep. Others migrate, or move to a warmer place for the season.

Hibernating Woodchuck in den

HIBERNATION

When a mammal hibernates, its heartbeat and breathing slow down, and its body temperature drops. It does not eat or drink but lives on fat stored in the body. A Woodchuck hibernates in its burrow for about six months. Its body temperature falls to only 40° Fahrenheit, and its heart beats just four times per minute.

Woodchuck (page 72) in autumn, eating to build up body fat for hibernation

DO BEARS HIBERNATE?

Like Woodchucks, Black Bears and Grizzlies prepare for winter by eating tremendous amounts of food to build up a layer of fat. Then they retire to winter dens and go to sleep. But bears do not truly hibernate. Their heart rate and body temperature drop only a little. They wake up several times during the winter and may even leave the den.

Black Bear (page 104) shortly after waking from winter sleep

Caribou (page 127) herd on migration

GETTING AWAY FROM IT ALL

Mammals migrate, or move from one place to another, mainly to escape bad weather (such as cold or drought) and to find food and water. In Alaska, herds of 100,000 or more Caribou follow routes used for thousands of years. They travel hundreds of miles between winter and summer feeding grounds as well as mating and birthing areas.

SEA TRAVEL

Gray Whales spend summer and early fall in the Arctic, then journey 5,000 miles south to Baja California, Mexico, where the calves are born. In spring the whales, including the new young, head north again.

Gray Whales   page 145

MOUNTAINEERING

Winter comes early in the western mountains. By late October, there may be several feet of snow in high forests and meadows. Elk, Mule Deer, and Bighorn Sheep remain at upper elevations for as long as possible, pawing through snow to find grasses and other plants. But eventually they must migrate down to winter grounds—open windswept slopes and meadows with less snow.

Bighorn Sheep (page 136) on winter feeding ground

Endangered species

Everything in the natural world is connected. A mammal shares its habitat with other animals and plants. Together they form an ecosystem. Mammals play many different roles in keeping ecosystems healthy. When a species—plant or animal—dies out, or becomes extinct, the entire ecosystem is affected.

West Indian Manatee page 142

A SPECIES IN TROUBLE

When an animal begins to die out, it is called endangered. It can become extinct if whatever is causing it to die out is not stopped. State wildlife officials in Florida are trying to save the endangered West Indian Manatee. This slow-moving, gentle mammal has suffered as human activities along rivers and waterways have destroyed many of its feeding and resting areas.

MAKING A DIFFERENCE!

The Blue Whale (pictured here) is not only the largest animal in the world today, it is also the largest animal that ever lived! By 1960, this incredible mammal had been hunted almost to extinction, and efforts were finally made to protect the species. Today its population is about 15,000. But the Blue Whale is still an endangered species, as are the Sperm Whale, the Gray Whale, the Humpback, and the Northern White. Restoring endangered species can take a long time. But the Blue Whale is proof that help makes a difference!

THREATENED AND ENDANGERED SPECIES

Below is a list of threatened (an animal that is in danger of becoming endangered is called threatened) and endangered mammals of North America. The list also shows the areas of North America where each species is in trouble.

SPECIES	LOCATION	STATUS
Grizzly Bear	U.S., except Alaska	Threatened
Mountain Lion	Canada to South America	Threatened
Bobcat	Entire range	Endangered
Caribou	Northern U.S., Canada	Endangered
Key Deer	Florida	Endangered
Black-footed Ferret	Western U.S., western Canada	Endangered
San Joaquin Kit Fox	California	Endangered
Jaguar	Southwestern U.S.	Endangered
West Indian Manatee	Southeastern U.S.	Endangered
Ocelot	Southwestern U.S.	Endangered
Virginia Northern Flying Squirrel	Virginia, West Virginia	Endangered
Blue Whale	Entire range	Endangered
Humpback Whale	Entire range	Endangered
Right Whale	Entire range	Endangered
Sperm Whale	Entire range	Endangered
Gray Wolf	U.S., except Minnesota	Endangered
Red Wolf	Entire range	Endangered

Habitat loss

Many things can endanger an animal, but the major cause is loss of the habitat an animal needs. Habitat loss is caused by the activities of people. Every day, habitats such as grasslands and forests are converted to farms, cities, and roadways. Outside of Alaska and Canada, Grizzly Bears survive in only a few western states. They require vast tracts of undisturbed land. Road building, timber harvesting, and house building are some of the reasons for their decline.

Where do mammals live?

Field guides like this one tell you two things about where a mammal lives: its range and its habitat. The range is the geographic area (such as the state or part of a country) where the animal lives. The habitat is the environment in which the animal lives. Deserts, woodlands, and marshes are habitats. A habitat contains the right combination of food, cover, and water a mammal needs to eat, sleep, hide from danger, and raise its young.

Marsh Rabbit

SPECIALISTS AND GENERALISTS

Some mammals are picky about where they live; others will live almost anywhere. An Eastern Cottontail will live in old fields and woodlands, near wetlands, and even in city parks and suburban areas. A Marsh Rabbit, on the other hand, will live only around swamps, lake edges, and coastal waters.

THE RANGE STORY

A mammal's range is the area in which the species is found. But the range tells you only part of the story—you also need to know the habitat. The American Beaver has a large range in North America, covering most of the United States and Canada. But you will find it only in the parts of North America that have its habitat: forested wetlands, ponds, rivers, and streams.

American Beaver habitat

American Beaver range

SIMILAR SPECIES, DIFFERENT HABITATS

Habitat needs are different for each species. The Red Fox and the Gray Fox look similar but they live in different habitats. The Red Fox lives in open meadows, grasslands, and pastures. The Gray Fox lives in forests and dense brushy areas. The habitat is the best clue for identifying these foxes.

Red Fox page 102

Gray Fox page 103

HOME ON THE RANGE

Most mammals have a home range, which is the area of its habitat that it lives in and feeds in. A mammal's home range may be large or small. A male Wolverine, for example, roams a vast home range—more than 1,000 miles. By contrast, the Thirteen-lined Ground Squirrel has a home range of no more than two or three acres.

Wolverine page 113

North American habitats

GRASSLANDS

Grasslands range from fields of tall grasses and wildflowers in areas with regular rainfall, to short-grass prairies in dry areas. Many grassland mammals sleep in underground burrows.

American Badger page 112

Grassland mammals: Pronghorn, Red Fox, Meadow Vole, Black-tailed Jackrabbit, American Badger, Black-tailed Prairie Dog, American Bison.

TUNDRA

The tundra is a wide-open plain stretching from northern Alaska and Canada to the polar ice caps. The ground is covered with a thick spongy mat of mosses and lichens. Winters are extremely cold and harsh; summers are brief.

Tundra mammals: Brown Lemming, Caribou, Grizzly Bear, Gray Wolf, Muskox, Arctic Fox.

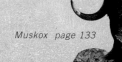

Muskox page 133

DESERTS

Deserts get very little rainfall. They are fiery hot during the day and cold at night. Mammals have adapted to life in the four deserts of the United States: the Sonoran, Chihuahuan, Great Basin, and Mojave.

Desert mammals: Collared Peccary, Desert Cottontail, Kit Fox, Desert Kangaroo Rat, Banner-tailed Kangaroo Rat, Pale Kangaroo Mouse.

Banner-tailed Kangaroo Rat page 87

Bighorn Sheep page 136

MOUNTAINS

Steep terrain, sparse vegetation, and harsh weather are part of life in high altitudes. Few mammals remain at the highest elevations all year; they either hibernate or seek sheltered valleys in winter. Mountain mammals: Elk, Bighorn Sheep, American Pika, Hoary Marmot, Mountain Goat, Mule Deer.

WOODLANDS

Forests attract many different types of mammals. Some, such as the Red Squirrel and the Gray Fox, spend all their time within a forest habitat. Others, such as the White-tailed Deer, Black Bear, and Bobcat, use forests for shelter and sleeping but feed and hunt in other habitats like meadows and wetlands.

Woodland mammals: Wolverine, Fisher, Virginia Opossum, Common Porcupine, Mountain Lion.

Common Porcupine page 96

SUBURBAN, URBAN AREAS

Living near roads, people, and buildings does not bother a number of mammals as long as they can find enough food, shelter, and water. Vacant lots, city parks, gardens, and backyards are home to many animals.

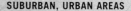

Eastern Gray Squirrel page 78

Urban and suburban mammals: Eastern Mole, Deer Mouse, Northern Short-tailed Shrew, Eastern Gray Squirrel, Common Raccoon, Eastern Chipmunk, Big Brown Bat.

STREAMS, LAKES, WETLANDS

The lush growth of grasses, shrubs, and trees surrounding marshes, ponds, lakes, streams, and rivers is important habitat for many mammals. Wetland mammals: Mink, American Beaver, Northern River Otter, Common Muskrat, Nutria, Star-nosed Mole.

Mink page 108

OCEANS AND SHORELINES

Oceans and shorelines provide a home to many mammals that are made for a watery life. Rugged, rocky seashores are especially appealing, providing good vantage points for fishing and lying in the sun, with fish and seaweeds just a short dive away.

Sperm Whale (page 147) tail

Ocean mammals: Sperm Whale, Humpback Whale, Killer Whale, Common Dolphin. Shoreline mammals: California Sea Lion, Gray Seal, Harbor Seal, Sea Otter, Northern Elephant Seal.

41

Detective work: trails, tracks, and other field signs

Think about how many wild birds you see each day—probably a dozen or more. How many wild mammals do you see in a day? One or two? Mammals are hard to see. Most are nocturnal (active only at night). All are shy; they usually flee at the first sign of danger. If you want to see mammals, you must learn to be a mammal detective. Begin by looking for field signs—clues to mammal activity.

Reading the signs

All mammals leave clues behind when they move around a place. Mammalogists call these clues a mammal's "signs." A good mammal detective learns to read these signs to identify many species and learn about their behavior and activities.

TRAILWAYS

Many mammals make trails through fields and forests as they go about their daily business. Deer roam around their home range on regular routes. Woodchucks go back and forth between one burrow entrance and another. Rabbits make paths of matted grass.

Pronghorn trail in grassland

TREE TALES

Trees give us many clues to mammal activity. Gnawed logs are signs of beavers in an area. In fall, male deer, Moose, and Elk scrape their antlers against tree trunks, leaving marks that are easy to see. Bears slash trees with their claws and teeth. Tree marking may be a form of communication between male and female bears since it usually occurs during mating season in summer.

Tree scarred by Elk antlers

HAIR AND THERE

When animals brush against trees, fences, or fallen logs, they often leave tufts of hair. Inspect the hair for color and texture. What animal might have left it?

Deer hair caught in barbed wire

BEDDING DOWN

Flattened grass in a field or clearing indicates that an animal has been sleeping there. Deer sometimes paw the snow away to reveal the leaves, which make a comfortable bed, underneath.

Deer's leaf bed in snow

HIDEOUTS

Woodchucks, foxes, badgers, and ground squirrels live in burrows or dens underground. A burrow entrance may be surrounded by a mound of dirt or may be under a rock or at the base of a tree.

Entrance to mouse den

43

PRACTICE MAKES PERFECT

To find mammals in the wild, you need to be in the right place at the right time. Early morning or dusk are good times to catch a glimpse of a nocturnal mammal (a mammal that is out at night) returning home or emerging from its shelter. With practice, you will be able to find mammals as well as their field signs. Try these tips:

- Start out in a place close to home, where you know your way around.
- Walk into the wind. Mammals have excellent noses and will move off as soon as they get your scent.
- Remain quiet. Take a few steps, then stop, look, and listen.
- Look for animals with your eyes first. Then, if you detect movement, use your binoculars.
- Do not spend all of your time walking. Find a comfortable spot like the base of a large tree. Sit down and relax. Let the animals come to you.

Moose scat

SCAT!

Animal droppings, called scat, are one of the easiest and best ways to identify mammals. The scat of each species is different. Moose scat looks like a bunch of small dark pellets. Wolf scat looks like the scat of a dog. Scat with porcupine quills in it is most likely from a Fisher, one of the few mammals that can eat the spiny creature.

MARKING TERRITORY

Some mammals, such as Mountain Lions and wolves, claim an area as their own territory. These animals often mark their territories with deposits of scat or sprays of urine. (You may see your pet dog or cat doing this.) Each animal's urine has its own scent that tells other animals that it has been there.

Gray Wolf (page 100) marking territory

Keeping track

In the field, look for mammal tracks in soft earth, mud, sand, or snow. The track drawings in the field guide will help you identify the animals that made them. Follow the tracks to see what kind of pattern they make. The track pattern can help you distinguish between species with similar tracks.

COYOTE

This is a Coyote track. Coyote tracks always show the claws. (Wildcat tracks do not always show claws because the claws can be pulled in.)

RACCOON

These are raccoon tracks. They look like small hands and print in pairs. In each pair the smaller front print is next to the larger back print.

FOX AND MOUSE

These are fox and mouse tracks. The fox tracks appear in almost single file.

MUSKRAT

These are muskrat tracks. The tail sometimes drags between the footprints.

45

Putting it all together

The field guide will help you to identify the mammals that you see. But how do you tell a Coyote from a Gray Wolf or a Mule Deer from a White-tailed Deer? The clues below will help you learn what sort of details to look for.

Mule Deer (page 125) antlers have two main branches on each side.

Color and markings

Even species that look alike have differences, often in their color and markings. It is easy to confuse ground squirrels with chipmunks in some western states. The best way to tell them apart is by markings: chipmunks have facial stripes; ground squirrels do not.

Least Chipmunk page 71

Golden-mantled Ground Squirrel page 75

Shape

Mammals often have a distinctive shape or profile. Some small mammals may look similar, but their shapes can help you identify them. For example, mice have rounded bodies, long tails, and big ears, while shrews have longer bodies, long, pointed noses, no visible ears, and short tails.

The Grizzly Bear (page 105) has a big hump above its shoulders; the Black Bear (page 104) does not.

The Black Bear's face looks straight and cone-shaped in profile, but the Grizzly's face curves inward slightly and is wider.

The Elk's (page 126) very large antlers have short branches growing forward over the face and larger ones growing over the back.

Special features

Horns and antlers look similar but are not the same. Horns, which grow on members of the cattle family, like Mountain Goats and Bighorn Sheep, remain on the head year-round. Antlers, worn by deer, are grown new each year and shed after the mating season.

The antlers of the White-tailed Deer (page 124) feature one main horizontal branch on each side, with smaller branches growing upward.

Red Fox page 102

Size

Size can help you identify animals that look similar. Beavers and muskrats may live in the same lake, but you will not mistake one for the other when you know that a beaver weighs up to 60 pounds, while the largest muskrat weighs no more than 4 pounds.

How can you tell foxes, Coyotes, and wolves apart? Check out the size. A Red Fox weighs about 8 to 15 pounds, a Coyote weighs 20 to 40, and a Gray Wolf weighs up to 130 pounds.

Coyote page 98

Gray Wolf page 100

Using the field guide

This section features 50 common North American mammals, plus 79 look-alikes, with photographs and descriptions of each. The mammals are mainly arranged in groups of related species called orders. The orders of land mammals covered are Opossums, Shrews and Moles, Bats, Armadillos, Rabbits, Rodents, Carnivores, and Hoofed Mammals. Marine Mammals (whales, dolphins, and seals) are grouped together at the end.

Black-tailed Prairie Dog
page 76

ICONS

These icons appear on each left-hand page in the field guide. They identify a mammal's general shape and grouping and tell you what order it is in.

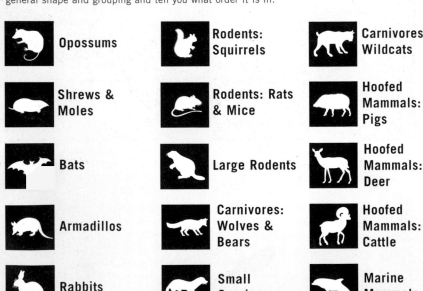

Opossums

Shrews & Moles

Bats

Armadillos

Rabbits

Rodents: Squirrels

Rodents: Rats & Mice

Large Rodents

Carnivores: Wolves & Bears

Small Carnivores

Carnivores: Wildcats

Hoofed Mammals: Pigs

Hoofed Mammals: Deer

Hoofed Mammals: Cattle

Marine Mammals

SHAPE ICON

This icon identifies the featured mammal's general shape and category.

NAME

The common and scientific names appear here.

TRACK DRAWINGS

These drawings show close-ups of tracks made by the front foot (left) and the rear foot (middle), with the measurement of each, as well as the pattern of the animal's tracks (right).

EASTERN COTTONTAIL
Sylvilagus floridanus

This common rabbit thrives in brush, abandoned farmlands, and suburbs. Mainly out at night, it can sometimes be seen around sunrise and sunset and on dark days. The Eastern Cottontail gives birth to several litters a year, with as many as seven young per litter. This helps keep the species from dying out, since it is preyed upon by many animals. A Red-tailed Hawk perched in a tree over brush is sometimes a good sign that a cottontail is nearby. **Look for:** A gray-brown rabbit with a white "cottontail," rusty orange fur behind its ears, and whitish feet. **Size:** Body 13–16" long, tail 2–3" long; 2–4 lb

Signs: Round front tracks and long hind tracks. Small, dark brown, round, pelletlike droppings. Bright orange urine in snow.

Habitat: Abandoned fields and brushy areas.

Range:

LOOK-ALIKES

DESERT COTTONTAIL
Sylvilagus auduboni
Look for: A small brown rabbit with a white belly and large ears. **Size:** Body 12–14" long. **Habitat:** Grasslands, dry brushy areas, and deserts. **Range:** Most southwestern and western states.

SWAMP RABBIT
Sylvilagus aquaticus
Look for: A very large water-loving rabbit, brownish gray with rust-colored feet. **Size:** Body 15–19" long (largest cottontail in North America). **Habitat:** Swamps, forested wetlands, and moist forests. **Range:** Deep southern states from Texas to South Carolina.

65

IDENTIFICATION CAPSULE

The identification capsule gives you the details you need to identify a mammal: color, size, parts of the body, and other field marks.

HABITAT AND RANGE

The range map and habitat listing tell you at a glance whether or not a mammal is likely to be seen in your area.

LOOK-ALIKES BOX

The look-alikes heading alerts you to other mammals covered in the box, which are similar to the main one on the page.

49

VIRGINIA OPOSSUM
Didelphis virginiana

The Virginia Opossum is a pouched mammal, like the kangaroos of Australia, giving birth to tiny hairless babies that live inside a pouch on the mother's belly before they are able to go out into the world. When frightened, opossums go into a trance and appear dead; this is called "playing possum."

LOOK FOR: A gray, furry, ratlike animal with a long hairless tail and a white face with a long snout.

SIZE: Body 15–19" long, tail 10–21" long; 4–14 lb.

SIGNS: Tracks look like hands; tail drags on ground between the feet; hind foot has a "thumb."

2"

2¼"

HABITAT: Farmlands, woodlands, and suburbs.

RANGE:

Although it is the largest shrew in North America and one of the most common mammals, the Northern Short-tailed Shrew is rarely seen. It spends much of its time tunneling under dead leaves on the forest floor, searching for insects, worms, and seeds. This species will fight over its territory, and sometimes a shrew that lost a fight will be found dead along a trail. This species tastes so bad, many other animals will not eat it.

LOOK FOR: A gray mouselike animal with a long slender snout and velvety fur. It has tiny eyes, no visible ears, and purple teeth. When running, its legs move so fast it looks like it is on wheels.

SIZE: Body 3–4" long, tail about 1" long; about 1 oz.

SIGNS: Series of short buzzing

sounds. Grass or leaf nests under a log.

HABITAT: Forests, grasslands, and stone walls.

RANGE:

CAUTION: Avoid touching this animal; its bite is not poisonous to humans but is very painful.

LEAST SHREW
Cryptotis parva
LOOK FOR: A tiny shrew with a cinnamon-brown back, gray belly, and short tail. **SIZE:** Body 2–3" long. **HABITAT:** Moist forests, fields, and marshes. **RANGE:** Most of eastern and midwestern U.S. and parts of Texas.

WATER SHREW
Sorex palustris
LOOK FOR: An almost black shrew with a light belly and a long tail. **SIZE:** Body 3–4" long. **HABITAT:** Mountain streams and lakeshore wetlands. **RANGE:** Most of Canada, southeastern Alaska, northern U.S., and Rocky Mts.

53

EASTERN MOLE
Scalopus aquaticus

The Eastern Mole lives almost its entire life underground. It feeds on earthworms, insect grubs, and other invertebrates, which it locates with its highly sensitive snout. Nests of dry grass and leaves, sometimes with a litter of babies, are occasionally found by people digging in their gardens.

LOOK FOR: A gray or brown mouselike animal with velvety fur, large wide forefeet, and a short naked tail.

SIZE: Body 3–8" long, tail about 1" long; 3–5 oz.

SIGNS: Molehills (piles of fresh dirt) and ridges made by tunneling.

HABITAT: Fields, lawns, and gardens.

RANGE:

BROAD-FOOTED MOLE
Scapanus latimanus
LOOK FOR: A brown or gray mole with a short hairy tail. **SIZE:** Body 4–6" long. **HABITAT:** Moist soil in a variety of habitats. **RANGE:** California and southern Oregon.

STAR-NOSED MOLE
Condylura cristata
LOOK FOR: A black mole with a cluster of pink, fleshy, fingerlike projections at the tip of the nose. **SIZE:** Body 4–5" long. **HABITAT:** Wetlands and moist woodlands. **RANGE:** Southeastern Canada, northeastern U.S., and parts of Midwest and Southeast.

FULL VIEW

LITTLE BROWN MYOTIS
Myotis lucifugus

It is too bad many people are afraid of bats, because they are amazing mammals and are usually harmless to humans. The Little Brown Myotis can fly, migrate, hibernate, sleep hanging upside-down, and find its way in the dark by echolocation. A single bat can eat 500 mosquitoes in an hour.

LOOK FOR: A small brown bat with short rounded ears and black wings, ears, and face.

SIZE: Body 2" long; ½ oz.

SIGNS: Mouselike droppings and a musty smell indoors. Sometimes a high-pitched "chirring" sound.

HABITAT: Near lakes and streams. Summer: mothers and young in buildings; winter: hibernates in caves.

RANGE:

CAUTION: Never handle bats; they can carry rabies, although they rarely attack humans.

HOARY BAT
Lasiurus cinereus
LOOK FOR: A large furry bat with a frosted appearance and an orange throat. **SIZE:** Body 3–4" long. **HABITAT:** Pine and leafy forests. **RANGE:** Southern Canada and throughout the U.S., except southern Florida.

BIG BROWN BAT
Eptesicus fuscus
LOOK FOR: A large brown bat with medium-size ears. **SIZE:** Body about 3" long. **HABITAT:** Forests, farmlands, cities, and parks. Summer and winter roosts are usually in buildings, not often in caves. **RANGE:** Southern Canada and throughout U.S., except southern Florida and southcentral Texas.

57

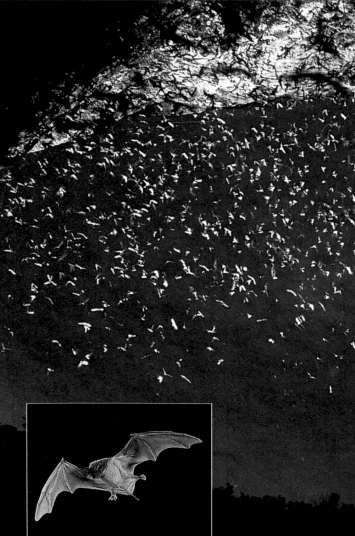

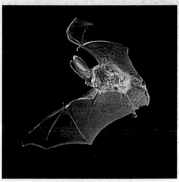

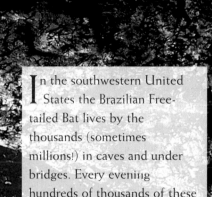

I n the southwestern United States the Brazilian Free-tailed Bat lives by the thousands (sometimes millions!) in caves and under bridges. Every evening hundreds of thousands of these bats fly out of Carlsbad Caverns in New Mexico. They feed all night on mosquitoes and other pesky insects.

LOOK FOR: A dark brown bat with a "free tail" not attached to a flap of skin.

SIZE: Body 2–3" long, tail about 1½" long; ½ oz.

SIGNS: Piles of brown droppings in caves and under bridges.

HABITAT: Farmlands and deserts. Roosts in caves, buildings, and under large bridges.

RANGE:

TOWNSEND'S BIG-EARED BAT
Plecotus townsendii

LOOK FOR: A medium-size bat with huge ears half the length of its body. Brown or gray back, tan belly. **SIZE:** Body about 3" long. **HABITAT:** Western deserts and dry pine forests, and eastern oak-hickory forests. **RANGE:** Mainly western U.S. to parts of Southwest.

EASTERN/WESTERN PIPISTRELLE
Pipistrellus subflavus/hesperus

LOOK FOR: A very small, light brown bat. **SIZE:** Body about 2" long. **HABITAT:** Eastern forests. **RANGE:** Eastern U.S. and parts of Midwest and Southwest.

NINE-BANDED ARMADILLO
Dasypus novemcinctus

Armadillos, or "armored ones" in Spanish, are the only mammals with a protective shell. It is made of heavy bony plates that cover the body. Armadillos might appear awkward or slow but they can move and dig quickly and can even swim. The Nine-banded Armadillo builds a nest in an underground den and ventures forth at night to dig for insects and other invertebrates. Its eyesight is so poor that you can sometimes get very close to an armadillo before it scoots away.

LOOK FOR: A round-backed animal with a brown, yellow, and tan shell and a pointed armored tail.

SIZE: Body 14–18" long, tail 10–15" long; 8–17 lb.

SIGNS: Birdlike tracks: 4 toes on the front and 5 on the back. Droppings look like clay marbles. Burrows have a 6–8" entrance.

1¾"

2⅛"

HABITAT: Forests and lowlands with moist soil and rotting wood where insects and other invertebrates live. Areas with sandy soil.

RANGE:

AMERICAN PIKA
Ochotona princeps

COLLARED PIKA
Ochotona collaris
LOOK FOR: An animal like the American Pika but gray on its sides, neck, and shoulders. No tail visible. **SIZE:** Body 7–8" long. **HABITAT:** Rocky slopes. **RANGE:** Southeastern Alaska and northwestern Canada.

The nickname "whistling hare" best describes this small rabbitlike animal with short round ears. Pikas live only in high elevation meadows in the Rocky Mountains. They are most easily found by their single-note whistle or bleat, then usually spotted perched on top of a rock with a good lookout. Instead of hibernating, they cut grass and build little haystacks among the rocks. When the hay is dry, they store it in underground dens for their winter food supply.

LOOK FOR: A small, brown, rabbitlike animal with low round ears. No tail visible.

SIZE: Body 7–8" long; 4–5 oz.

SIGNS: Droppings are small, round, and black. Loud whistle.

HABITAT: Rocky hillsides over 8,000' high.

RANGE:

EASTERN COTTONTAIL
Sylvilagus floridanus

This common rabbit thrives in brush, abandoned farmlands, and suburbs. Mainly out at night, it can sometimes be seen around sunrise and sunset and on dark days. The Eastern Cottontail gives birth to several litters a year, with as many as seven young per litter. This helps keep the species from dying out, since it is preyed upon by many animals. A Red-tailed Hawk perched in a tree over brush is sometimes a good sign that a cottontail is nearby.

LOOK FOR: A gray-brown rabbit with a white "cottontail," rusty orange fur behind its ears, and whitish feet.

SIZE: Body 13–16" long, tail 2–3" long; 2–4 lb.

SIGNS: Round front tracks and long hind tracks. Small, dark brown, round, pelletlike droppings. Bright orange urine in snow.

HABITAT: Abandoned fields and brushy areas.

RANGE:

DESERT COTTONTAIL
Sylvilagus audubonii

LOOK FOR: A small brown rabbit with a white belly and large ears. **SIZE:** Body 12–14" long. **HABITAT:** Grasslands, dry brushy areas, and deserts. **RANGE:** Most southwestern and western states.

SWAMP RABBIT
Sylvilagus aquaticus

LOOK FOR: A very large water-loving rabbit, brownish gray with rust-colored feet. **SIZE:** Body 15–19" long (largest cottontail in North America). **HABITAT:** Swamps, forested wetlands, and moist forests. **RANGE:** Deep southern states from Texas to South Carolina.

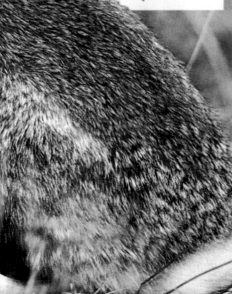

65

SNOWSHOE HARE
Lepus americanus

WINTER COAT

ARCTIC HARE
Lepus arcticus

LOOK FOR: A large hare with a gray-brown coat in summer or a white coat in winter. In northernmost areas the coat is white year-round. Short black-tipped ears. **SIZE:** Body 17–24" long. **HABITAT:** Rocky areas and tundras. **RANGE:** Northern Canada.

Who really invented snowshoes? Early Native Americans were masters at observing nature and most likely got the idea from the Snowshoe Hare. These large rabbits are well suited for their environment. The color of their coat changes seasonally to help them hide against predators. They shed their brown summer coat for a white winter coat. They are also unusual in that they have a nine-year population cycle that brings them from extreme abundance to near disappearance.

LOOK FOR: A hare with a white coat in winter or a brown coat in summer. It has large white hind feet that look like snowshoes.

SIZE: Body 14–18" long, tail 1–2" long; 2–3 lb.

SIGNS: Large hind tracks. Pathways in snow. Droppings are large flattened pellets.

1½"

4–5"

HABITAT: Northern spruce-fir forests and balsam swamps.

RANGE:

Black-tailed Jackrabbit
Lepus californicus

The Black-tailed Jackrabbit may look silly with its enormous "donkey" ears, long legs, and big feet, but it is well suited to its harsh environment. Mammals that live in hot climates can cool themselves by releasing heat through their long thin ears, slender legs, and big feet.

Look for: A large, fast, gray-brown rabbit with enormous ears and a black-striped tail and rump.

Size: Body 16–21" long, tail 2–4" long; 4–8 lb.

Signs: Large tracks on worn packed trails. Droppings are large round brown pellets.

1½"

2½"

Habitat: Short-grass prairies, mountain meadows, and farmlands.

Range:

WHITE-TAILED JACKRABBIT
Lepus townsendii

LOOK FOR: A gray-white jackrabbit with long ears and legs and a white tail. **SIZE:** Body 20–22" long. **HABITAT:** Grasslands and farmlands. **RANGE:** Western states, but south only to Utah, Colorado, and Kansas, and east to Minnesota and Iowa.

ANTELOPE JACKRABBIT
Lepus alleni

LOOK FOR: A leaping gray-brown jackrabbit with very long ears. **SIZE:** Body 20–23" long. **HABITAT:** Mostly grassy slopes but also deserts. **RANGE:** South-central Arizona.

69

EASTERN CHIPMUNK
Tamias striatus

Eastern Chipmunks are active by day and always on the move,
constantly gathering seeds, nuts, and acorns to store for the winter.
Unlike most other hibernators, chipmunks wake up frequently to eat
food stored in their underground dens. They will sometimes come above
ground on a warm winter day.

LOOK FOR: A small reddish-brown rodent with one white stripe on each side that is bordered in black.

SIZE: Body 5–7" long, tail 3–4" long; 2–5 oz.

SIGNS: Tracks are seldom seen in snow but look like small squirrel tracks in mud. Chewed nutshells on stone walls and logs. A quick "chip-chip-chip" as they run down a hole or a continuous low-pitched "chuck-chuck-chuck."

HABITAT: Leafy forests, brushy areas, stone walls, and suburbs.

RANGE:

LEAST CHIPMUNK
Tamias minimus

LOOK FOR: A small grayish chipmunk with dark stripes and a long black-tipped tail. **SIZE:** Body 4–5" long **HABITAT:** Pine forests and sagebrush in rocky areas. **RANGE:** Western and southern Canada to Wisconsin, south through Rocky Mts. into New Mexico.

YELLOW-PINE CHIPMUNK
Tamias amoenus

LOOK FOR: A brightly colored chipmunk with bold stripes on face. **SIZE:** Body 4–5" long. **HABITAT:** Brushy areas in yellow-pine forests. **RANGE:** Western Canada south through northern Rocky Mts.

71

WOODCHUCK/GROUNDHOG
Marmota monax

Woodchucks, celebrated every February on Groundhog Day, cannot really forecast the end of winter. However, these oversize squirrels can do other amazing things, like swim, climb trees, and whistle. They dig large underground dens that later might become home to skunks, rabbits, raccoons, or other small mammals.

LOOK FOR: A very large ground mammal with short legs, coarse brown fur sprinkled with gray, and a bushy black tail.

SIZE: Body 13–26" long, tail 4–6" long; 5–14 lb.

SIGNS: A large burrow entrance from 8–11" wide with fresh dirt at the front or on the downhill side. Alarm call: single, loud, clear whistle.

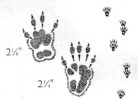

2⅛"

2¾"

HABITAT: Hay fields, pastures, and meadows with woods nearby for winter dens. Found where soil is loose and pebbly.

RANGE:

YELLOW-BELLIED MARMOT
Marmota flaviventris

LOOK FOR: An animal like a Woodchuck but with yellowish-brown fur and a yellow belly. **SIZE:** Body 13–20" long. **HABITAT:** High-elevation mountain meadows with rocky areas. **RANGE:** Southwest Canada to western U.S.

HOARY MARMOT
Marmota caligata

LOOK FOR: A big Woodchuck with silver hair and black markings on head and shoulders. **SIZE:** Body 11–22" long. **HABITAT:** High mountain meadows with rocky areas. **RANGE:** Alaska and western Canada south to Washington, Idaho, and Montana.

THIRTEEN-LINED GROUND SQUIRREL
Spermophilus tridecemlineatus

These ground squirrels, named for their bold pattern, live in grassy areas throughout central North America. They eat plant seeds, grasshoppers, and crickets. Thirteen-lined Ground Squirrels are easy to spot because they are active during the day and often stand straight up to look around.

LOOK FOR: A tan ground squirrel with 13 brown-and-white stripes broken up into spots along its back and sides.

SIZE: Body 5–6" long, tail 2–5" long; 4–10 oz.

SIGNS: A hole or burrow entrance with many little pathways leading away from it.

HABITAT: Pastures, lawns, and other short grassy areas.

RANGE:

GOLDEN-MANTLED GROUND SQUIRREL
Spermophilus lateralis

LOOK FOR: A ground squirrel with a reddish head and shoulders and a white stripe with black stripes on each side. **SIZE:** Body 6–8" long. **HABITAT:** Pine forests and brushy areas. **RANGE:** Mountains of western Canada and U.S.

WHITE-TAILED ANTELOPE SQUIRREL
Ammospermophilus leucurus

LOOK FOR: A ground squirrel with white side stripes. Body brownish yellow in summer and gray in winter. Tail white underneath. **SIZE:** Body 5–6" long. **HABITAT:** Deserts and at the foot of hills and mountains. **RANGE:** Oregon, Idaho, California, Nevada, Utah, Arizona, Colorado, and New Mexico.

BLACK-TAILED PRAIRIE DOG
Cynomys ludovicianus

These prairie dogs, the only species with a black tip on the tail, build vast prairie-dog towns. They were nearly poisoned out in the early days of ranching because they eat a lot of grass and because cattle and horses can break a leg in their holes.

LOOK FOR: A large ground squirrel with a light brown back, white belly, and thin, black-tipped tail.

SIZE: Body 10–11" long, tail 3–5" long; 2½–4 lb.

SIGNS: A big prairie-dog town with high mounds of hard-packed dirt at each entrance.

1¼"

1¼"

HABITAT: Short-grass prairies.

RANGE:

WHITE-TAILED PRAIRIE DOG
Cynomys leucurus

LOOK FOR: A prairie dog with a short white-tipped tail. Yellow nose and small ears. **SIZE:** Body about 12" long. **HABITAT:** High-elevation sagebrush plains. **RANGE:** Parts of Wyoming, Colorado, and Utah.

UTAH PRAIRIE DOG
Cynomys parvidens

LOOK FOR: A prairie dog very similar to the White-tailed but slightly redder. **SIZE:** Body 11–12" long. **HABITAT:** Short-grass prairies. **RANGE:** South-central Utah.

EASTERN GRAY SQUIRREL
Sciurus carolinensis

Many things in nature are related and interconnected. These familar squirrels live in eastern leafy forests and eat a lot of hickory nuts, acorns, walnuts, maple seeds, and beechnuts. One of the ways they store food for winter is to bury a nut here and there so deer and turkeys do not eat them all. Of course the squirrels cannot find every nut they bury. In this way, they actually plant the trees and build the forests that feed them.

RED SQUIRREL
Tamiasciurus hudsonicus

LOOK FOR: A small, very active, reddish-brown tree squirrel. Highly territorial and very vocal. **SIZE:** Body 7–9" long. **HABITAT:** Pine forests. **RANGE:** Most of Alaska, Canada, Rocky Mts., and Northeast.

ABERT'S SQUIRREL
Sciurus aberti

LOOK FOR: A gray tree squirrel sprinkled with white with big tufts of fur on ears. Makes nest of pine twigs. **SIZE:** Body 11–13" long. **HABITAT:** Yellow or ponderosa pine forests. **RANGE:** Parts of Southwest.

NORTHERN/SOUTHERN FLYING SQUIRREL
Glaucomys sabrinus/volans

LOOK FOR: A small nocturnal squirrel with soft velvety brown fur and big black eyes. **SIZE:** Body 5–7" long. **HABITAT:** Pine forests. **RANGE:** Most of Canada, eastern half of U.S., and parts of West.

LOOK FOR: A large tree squirrel, usually gray but sometimes brown or black, with a big bushy tail.

SIZE: Body 9–10" long, tail 8–9" long; 14–25 oz.

SIGNS: Tracks most visible in snow. Chewed nuts on the ground. Leaf nests in trees.

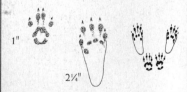

1"

2¼"

HABITAT: Leafy forests with nut-bearing trees like oak, hickory, beech, and walnut.

RANGE:

BOTTA'S POCKET GOPHER
Thomomys bottae

Pocket gophers live underground and often match the color of the soil they live in. These rodents are named for the two pouches in their cheeks where they store food as they tunnel along. When they get back to their nest, they empty their cheek "pockets" of the tasty stems and roots they have collected.

LOOK FOR: A brown rodent with small eyes and ears, large front claws, big front teeth, and a long tail.

SIZE: Body about 5–7" long; tail 2–3" long; 5 oz.

SIGNS: Fresh dirt in a line and mounds of soil.

NORTHERN POCKET GOPHER
Thomomys talpoides

LOOK FOR: A typical pocket gopher. **SIZE:** Body 6" long. **HABITAT:** Mountain meadows. **RANGE:** Southern Canada and western U.S.

WESTERN POCKET GOPHER
Geomys pinetis

LOOK FOR: A typical pocket gopher. **SIZE:** Body 6" long. **HABITAT:** Pastures and fields. **RANGE:** Washington, Oregon, and California.

1–1½"

1–1½"

HABITAT: Various habitats, from deserts to mountain meadows.

RANGE:

DEER MOUSE
Peromyscus maniculatus

This common mouse with big sparkling eyes lives in many habitats and comes in many colors. The Deer Mouse eats seeds, nuts, fruits, insects, and fungi. It often lives in trees and old bird nests. In the fall, it may come into houses, but it does not cause as many problems as the House Mouse. As with all mice, many predators feed on it.

LOOK FOR: A gray to reddish-brown mouse with a white belly and a very long tail.

SIZE: Body 3–4" long, tail 2–5" long; about 1 oz.

SIGNS: Tracks in snow may show tail dragging between footprints. Nests in trees, hollow logs, or burrows.

¼"   ⅝"

HABITAT: Woodlands, fields, grasslands, and prairies.

RANGE:

WHITE-FOOTED MOUSE
Peromyscus leucopus

LOOK FOR: A golden-brown mouse with a white belly and long gray tail. **SIZE:** Body 3–4" long. **HABITAT:** Brushy areas and woodlands. **RANGE:** Eastern U.S. (except South), Midwest, Southwest, and parts of West.

NORTHERN GRASSHOPPER MOUSE
Onychomys leucogaster

LOOK FOR: A mouse like the Deer Mouse but with a shorter thicker tail with white tip. **SIZE:** Body 4–5" long. **HABITAT:** Low valleys, deserts, and prairies. **RANGE:** Southern Canada and western U.S.

BRUSH MOUSE
Peromyscus boylii

LOOK FOR: A brown mouse like the Deer Mouse but with a longer tail. **SIZE:** Body 4–5" long. **HABITAT:** Brushy areas. **RANGE:** California and southwestern U.S.

83

HOUSE MOUSE
Mus musculus

This pesky little mouse came to the New World with early explorers and has spread throughout North America. The House Mouse lives in farmlands and in buildings and causes a lot of damage by chewing or shredding things. It also contaminates food and grain with its droppings.

LOOK FOR: A grayish-brown mouse with a dark gray belly and a long hairless tail.

SIZE: Body 3–4" long, tail 3–4" long; about ¾ oz.

SIGNS: Small, dark, rice-shaped droppings. Shredded nesting materials and chewed holes in woodwork.

HABITAT: Buildings and farms.

RANGE:

WESTERN HARVEST MOUSE
Reithrodontomys megalotis

LOOK FOR: A small brown mouse with a white belly. Makes round grass nest. **SIZE:** Body 3" long. **HABITAT:** Grassy areas, marshes, deserts, and oak and pine forests. **RANGE:** Western and central U.S.

MEADOW JUMPING MOUSE
Zapus hudsonius

LOOK FOR: A brown mouse with huge hind feet. **SIZE:** Body 3–4" long. **HABITAT:** Meadows and brushy areas. **RANGE:** Canada and northeastern U.S.

GREAT BASIN POCKET MOUSE
Perognathus parvus

LOOK FOR: A small mouse with a furry tail. **SIZE:** Body 3" long. **HABITAT:** Dry plains. **RANGE:** Western U.S.

ORD'S KANGAROO RAT
Dipodomys ordii

Like little kangaroos, these nocturnal rats hop about on their long powerful legs, using their tails for balance. They build well-designed underground tunnels and nest chambers with small entrances, which they plug up to control temperature and moisture.

Look for: A light brown rat with a long black-and-white tail with a tuft of fur at the tip and very large, 5-toed hind feet.

Size: Body 4–5" long, tail 4–6" long; 2–3 oz.

Signs: Distinctive tracks with small front feet between hind feet. Tail leaves a long drag mark. Small burrow openings in the center of a dirt mound.

½"

1½"

Habitat: Deserts or sandy dry areas.

Range:

PALE KANGAROO MOUSE
Microdipodops pallidus

Look for: A small, light brown kangaroo mouse with a thick tail that has no tuft or distinct markings. **Size:** Body about 3" long. **Habitat:** Deserts. **Range:** Sonoran Desert of Nevada and California.

DESERT KANGAROO RAT
Dipodomys deserti

Look for: A large tan kangaroo rat with 4 toes on the hind feet. Tail has a grayish band just before the white tip. **Size:** Body 5–6" long. **Habitat:** Brushy sandy areas. **Range:** Southwestern U.S.

BANNER-TAILED KANGAROO RAT
Dipodomys spectabilis

Look for: A large yellowish-brown kangaroo rat with a black band before a white tip on the tail and 4 toes on the hind feet. **Size:** Body 5–6" long. **Habitat:** Deserts, grasslands, and brushy areas. **Range:** Southwestern U.S.

NORWAY RAT
Rattus norvegicus

Some animals have benefited from human activities, and the Norway Rat seems to be at the top of that list. Farming, building cities, and storing grain are the types of activities that have helped rats spread throughout the world. At one time, a deadly disease known as the black plague, carried by rats and their fleas, killed many people in Europe, but today antibiotics have nearly eliminated that problem.

LOOK FOR: A brownish-gray rat with a hairless tail.

SIZE: Body 8–10" long, tail 5–9" long; 7–17 oz.

SIGNS: Tracks with tail drags between feet. Heel of hind foot often does not print. Droppings are dark pellets ½" long. Nests of shredded paper, clothing and cardboard. Round chewed holes in walls.

¾"

1⅝"

HABITAT: Cities, buildings, and farmlands.

RANGE:

BUSHY-TAILED WOODRAT
Neotoma cinerea

LOOK FOR: A brown rat sprinkled with black with big ears and a bushy tail like a squirrel. **SIZE:** Body 7–9" long. **HABITAT:** Rocky areas in pine forests. **RANGE:** Yukon south through western U.S. to New Mexico and Arizona.

BLACK RAT
Rattus rattus

LOOK FOR: A gray, brown, or blackish rat with big ears and a longer tail than the Norway Rat. **SIZE:** Body 6–8" long. **HABITAT:** Seaports and buildings. **RANGE:** Southern and coastal U.S.

HISPID COTTON RAT
Sigmodon hispidus

LOOK FOR: A small, dark brown rat sprinkled with tan with a scaly tail. **SIZE:** Body 5–8" long. **HABITAT:** Grassy and weedy areas. **RANGE:** Southern U.S.

MEADOW VOLE
Microtus pennsylvanicus

With its short legs and short tail, the Meadow Vole looks part hamster and part mouse. Often called field mice, Meadow Voles tunnel under the grass in hayfields, meadows, and grassy strips along roads. They are preyed upon by many predators but keep their numbers up by having litters every month of the year.

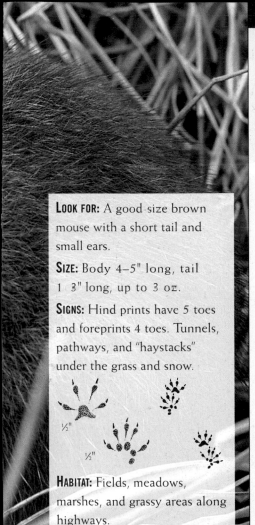

LOOK FOR: A good size brown mouse with a short tail and small ears.

SIZE: Body 4–5" long, tail 1 3" long, up to 3 oz.

SIGNS: Hind prints have 5 toes and foreprints 4 toes. Tunnels, pathways, and "haystacks" under the grass and snow.

½"

½"

HABITAT: Fields, meadows, marshes, and grassy areas along highways.

RANGE:

WOODLAND VOLE
Microtus pinetorum

LOOK FOR: A small reddish-brown mouse with a tan belly and a very short tail. **SIZE:** Body 4–5" long. **HABITAT:** Leafy woodlands with deep layers of leaves or grass on the ground. **RANGE:** Eastern U.S. from Iowa to Atlantic Coast, except for most of Maine and Florida.

BROWN LEMMING
Synaptomys cooperi

LOOK FOR: A small brown hamsterlike mouse with a very short tail. Makes grass nests about 7" wide. **SIZE:** Body 4–5" long. **HABITAT:** Tundra and mountains. **RANGE:** Alaska and northern and western Canada.

AMERICAN BEAVER
Castor canadensis

A merican Beavers construct valuable wildlife habitats. They dam streams, creating ponds that support fish, frogs, turtles, waterfowl, muskrats, Minks, otters, and Moose. Trees drowned by the rising water provide nest sites for woodpeckers, tree swallows, Ospreys, and herons. Over time the ponds fill in with sediment and become wet meadows for deer, Elk, rabbits, and voles.

LOOK FOR: A large reddish-brown rodent with a black paddle-shaped tail. Best seen on summer evenings around its lodge or dam or on the shore. Makes a big V on the water when it swims.

SIZE: Body 24–36" long, tail 12–18" long; 44–60 lb.

SIGNS: Flooded areas, dams and lodges built of sticks, felled trees, and gnawed and peeled sticks. Loud tail smacks on the water.

3"

6½"

RANGE:

HABITAT: Forested wetlands, ponds, marshes, rivers, and streams.

CAUTION: Never drink water from beaver ponds; they carry parasites.

COMMON MUSKRAT
Ondatra zibethicus

Common Muskrats eat so much marsh vegetation that they create open water and new habitat for waterfowl. These aquatic rodents build miniature lodges, like those of beavers, but use cattails instead of trees.

LOOK FOR: A glossy reddish-brown rodent with a long, pointed, almost hairless tail. Usually hunched up on the shoreline or swimming. Like a beaver, it cuts a V in the water with its head when swimming, but the muskrat swings its tail from side to side or arches it upward with the edge out of the water.

SIZE: Body 9–12" long, tail 7–12" long; 1–4 lb.

SIGNS: Droppings ½" long on logs and rocks just above the waterline. Lodges and feeding platforms built of cattails and grasses and clipped vegetation floating near shore. Makes tunnels and runways in marsh.

1¼"

2"

COYOTE
Canis latrans

LOOK FOR: A large, nearly round rodent covered with long quills. Western porcupines appear yellow; those in the East are dark brown to black.

SIZE: Body 20–25" long, tail 6–12" long; 8–40 lb.

SIGNS: Piles of droppings at base of tree or cave entrance. Odor like chicken soup. Gnawed bark and twigs. Well-worn footpaths. Various grunts, whines, and whistles.

3"

3½"

HABITAT: Pine and leafy forests (especially with rock ledges for dens) in the East and dry brushy areas in the West.

RANGE:

COMMON PORCUPINE
Erethizon dorsatum

This unmistakable animal eats bark high in trees during winter, then shifts to plants on the ground in summer. Its quills are a good defense but do not keep all animals away. Fishers and Mountain Lions eat porcupines with little trouble. Although Common Porcupines cannot really shoot their quills, be very careful around them. They can swing their tails much farther, faster, and harder than you might expect. Dogs never seem to learn to keep away from them and are often injured.

HABITAT: Marshes, lakes, ponds, rivers, and streams.

RANGE:

NUTRIA
Myocastor coypus

LOOK FOR: A large brown aquatic rodent with a long round tail. Lives in marshes but makes a burrow in the bank, not a lodge. Often grunts loudly, like a pig, at dusk. **SIZE:** Body 12–36" long. **HABITAT:** Streams, ponds, and marshes. **RANGE:** Mostly in the lower Mississippi River area, but scattered colonies north to New Jersey. Also in Washington and Oregon.

The clever Coyote or "the trickster," as some Native American tribes called it, may be one of the most intelligent and successful mammals in North America. While many efforts were made to get rid of them in the West, they seem to have increased and spread their range into the East. Historical records describe smaller "Brush Wolves" that may have been Coyotes. So the trickster can even fool the scientists attempting to study it.

LOOK FOR: A harmless, gray or orange-gray, doglike animal with a black-tipped bushy tail that hangs low.

SIZE: Body about 3' long, tail 12–15" long, 20–40 lb.

SIGNS: Doglike droppings that contain hair. Very vocal: barks and yelps followed by a long howl and short yaps.

HABITAT: Brushy areas in the East and open plains in the West.

RANGE:

GRAY WOLF
Canis lupus

LOOK FOR: A large German Shepherd-like canine with a long bushy black-tipped tail. Usually gray, but color varies from white to black.

SIZE: Body 3–5' long, tail 14–20" long; 57–130 lb.

SIGNS: Doglike tracks in a straight line, usually in wilderness areas where there are no dogs. Twisted droppings containing remains of prey, mostly hair. Makes a great variety of calls and choruses.

4¾"   4¾"

HABITAT: Northern forests and tundras.

RANGE:

Once feared and hated, today the Gray Wolf is a beloved symbol of the wilderness. In spite of all the stories, there have only been three recorded instances of wolves attacking humans in North America, and none of the attacks were deadly. However, wolves hunt in packs and can kill cattle as well as deer, Caribou, and Moose.

RED WOLF
Canis rufus

LOOK FOR: A smaller southern wolf. Reddish-brown to gray. Usually in pairs that form temporary packs. **SIZE:** Body 3–4' long. **HABITAT:** Southern prairies, swamps, and brushy areas. **RANGE:** Southwestern Texas and southeastern Louisiana. Once nearly extinct but now reintroduced to other areas of the South.

RED FOX
Vulpes vulpes

LOOK FOR: A rusty-red fox with black legs and a bushy long tail tipped in white. Some Red Foxes are black, silver, or a red-and-black mix.

SIZE: Body about 24" long, tail 14–17" long; 8–15 lb.

SIGNS: Tracks in a straight line like a cat's, but claws show. Droppings small, dark, and pointed. They often contain fur, seeds, or beetle-wing covers.

2½"

2½"

HABITAT: Woodlands, hay fields, brushy areas, pastures, and parks.

RANGE:

CAUTION: Foxes carry rabies and distemper, so look but do not touch.

The sight of a handsome Red Fox against a new fallen snow on a bright winter day will stay with you forever. These foxes are indeed sly, for such a sight is uncommon, even though their tracks reveal their presence almost everywhere. They eat a variety of foods but mainly live on rabbits and voles in winter, shifting to fruits and insects in summer.

GRAY FOX
Urocyon cinereoargenteus

LOOK FOR: A gray fox with a black-and-white face and red around the ears, neck, chest, and lower sides. Tail black on top and at tip. **SIZE:** Body 24" long. **HABITAT:** Woodlands and brushy areas. **RANGE:** Most of the U.S., but not in Rockies or parts of Great Plains.

KIT FOX
Vulpes velox

LOOK FOR: A small fox similar to the Gray Fox but paler and less red with larger ears and white legs. **SIZE:** Body 15–19" long. **HABITAT:** Prairies, deserts, and sagebrush. **RANGE:** South-central Canada and western and central U.S.

ARCTIC FOX
Alopex lagopus

LOOK FOR: A fox of the extreme north, pure white in winter, brownish-gray in summer. **SIZE:** Body 19–22" long. **HABITAT:** Tundras and sea ice. **RANGE:** Alaska and northern Canada.

103

BLACK BEAR
Ursus americanus

Black Bears are more and more common in the eastern United States, where they are learning to live at the edges of suburbs. They are not dangerous as long as you keep away from them. Although they are carnivores, Black Bears eat very little meat. Instead, they live on grasses and other plants in spring, fruits and berries in summer, and nuts and acorns in fall. Black Bears head for a den in October and sleep much of the winter but they do not enter the deep phase of true hibernation.

GRIZZLY BEAR
Ursus arctos

LOOK FOR: A large brown bear usually with white-tipped hairs. **SIZE:** Body 6–7' long. **HABITAT:** Mountain meadows and forests; along streams and rivers (especially those with salmon runs); berry bushes or willow thickets. Avoid these habitats in bear country. **RANGE:** Alaska and Canada south to Wyoming in Rocky Mts. **CAUTION:** Grizzlies are one of the most dangerous animals. Do not get within ½ mile of one; they are very fast and will attack people.

POLAR BEAR
Ursus maritimus

LOOK FOR: A large white bear with a long neck and small ears. **SIZE:** Body 7–11' long. **HABITAT:** In and about waters where seals are plentiful. Sometimes seen on tundras, but never too far inland. **RANGE:** Arctic Canada and Alaska.

LOOK FOR: A large black long-legged bear. Moves much faster than you might think

SIZE: Body 4–6' long, 3–4' high; tail 3–7" long; 200–600 lb.

SIGNS: Droppings usually dark brown or black, cylindrical, like a dog's but bigger. Often found along a trail, droppings frequently contain beetle fragments, grass in spring, and berry seeds in summer. Other signs are rotten logs torn open and claw marks on trees.

6"

7"

HABITAT: Forests, swamps, and parklands near eastern suburbs.

RANGE:

COMMON RACCOON
Procyon lotor

LOOK FOR: A gray nocturnal animal with a black face mask and a bushy ringed tail.

SIZE: Body 16–21" long, tail 8–16" long; 12–48 lb.

SIGNS: Tracks like small hands. Droppings like a dog's but packed with seeds and crayfish shells. Often found at the base of a tree.

3"

3¾"

HABITAT: Woodlands, riverbanks, wetlands, and suburbs.

The mischievous raccoon, famous for its nighttime raids on trash cans, can find a home most anywhere, from woodlands to suburbs. Its secret to success lies in its intelligence, agile hands, and ability to eat a variety of foods. Raccoons can be vicious predators on small animals, from chickens to kittens.

RINGTAIL
Bassariscus astutus

LOOK FOR: A nocturnal foxlike animal with big brown eyes, a light yellowish-brown coat, and a long, bushy, black-banded tail. **SIZE:** Body 12–15″ long. **HABITAT:** Rocky areas in desert and brush. **RANGE:** California, Oregon, Nevada, Utah, Colorado, and all of the Southwest.

WHITE-NOSED COATI
Nasua narica

LOOK FOR: A dog-size brown animal with a long pointed snout and a long tail. Active during the day. **SIZE:** Body 17–26″ long. **HABITAT:** Forests and wooded canyons near water. **RANGE:** Arizona, New Mexico, and Texas along Mexican border.

RANGE:

CAUTION: Raccoons can carry rabies, so never get close to one.

107

MINK
Mustela vison

Minks are known for their rich glossy fur. These highly aggressive predators live a solitary nocturnal lifestyle and prey on a wide variety of animals. The larger males kill muskrats and rabbits while the smaller females go after mice and songbirds. Both sexes eat a lot of fish, frogs, and crayfish. They inhabit all types of wetlands but freshwater swamps and marshy lakeshores are preferred.

LOOK FOR: A rich brown or glossy black animal with a white chin. Most often seen bounding along a freshwater shoreline.

SIZE: Body 13–20" long, tail 6–7" long; 2–4 lb.

SIGNS: Round tracks often found along the water's edge. Droppings are dark and cylindrical and may contain fur or bone.

1¾"

1¾"

HABITAT: Wetlands, rivers, and shorelines.

RANGE:

AMERICAN MARTEN
Martes americana

LOOK FOR: A large brown tree-dwelling animal with a foxlike face, orange throat patch, and bushy tail. **SIZE:** Body 14–18" long. **HABITAT:** Northern pine forests. **RANGE:** Most of Canada and south to California, Rocky Mts., Great Lakes region, and New England.

FISHER
Martes pennanti

LOOK FOR: An animal similar to the marten but larger and darker. Eats porcupines; droppings often contain quills. **SIZE:** Body 19–24" long. **HABITAT:** Northern pine forests. **RANGE:** Southern half of Canada south to parts of California, Rocky Mts., Utah, New York, and New England.

109

LONG-TAILED WEASEL
Mustela frenata

LOOK FOR: A long, slim, very active animal with short legs and a long black-tipped tail. Usually brown in summer, white in winter.

SIZE: Body 8–16" long, tail 3–6" long; 3–9 oz.

SIGNS: Because weasels usually leap or run rather than walk, all 4 footprints are usually in a cluster.

1"

1¾"

AMERICAN BADGER
Taxidea taxus

Badgers are solitary predators whose specialty is digging out ground squirrels, prairie dogs, and other burrowing animals. They have long curved claws on short powerful legs and can dig with amazing speed.

LOOK FOR: A short, wide, flattened animal with a black-and-white face, and a gray or brown coat of coarse fur with some white mixed in.

SIZE: Body 16–28" long, tail 4–6" long; 8–25 lb.

SIGNS: Dens with large oval openings and mounds of soil with bones scattered about the entrance.

These slim little predators hunt a variety of prey, from rabbits and chickens to mice and frogs. If any animal can be called bloodthirsty, the weasel may qualify because it kills its victim by biting into the base of the head and drinking the blood. Weasels often kill far more than they can eat. If they manage to gain entry to a hen house or a pigeon coop, they go wild.

HABITAT: Forests, fields, and brushy areas.

RANGE:

SHORT-TAILED WEASEL
Mustela erminea

LOOK FOR: A brownish-gray weasel smaller than the Long-tailed and with white feet. **SIZE:** Body 6–10" long. **HABITAT:** Forests, grasslands, brushy areas, and wetlands. **RANGE:** Alaska, most of Canada, and south to parts of the West, Midwest, and Northeast.

BLACK-FOOTED FERRET
Mustela nigripes

LOOK FOR: A very large tan weasel with a black face mask. Nearly extinct. **SIZE:** Body 15–18" long. **HABITAT:** Prairie-dog towns in dry western prairies. **RANGE:** Parts of Montana, Wyoming, South Dakota, and Nebraska.

LEAST WEASEL
Mustela nivalis

LOOK FOR: A very small brownish weasel with white neck, belly, and feet and a short tail. **SIZE:** Body 6–7" long. **HABITAT:** Fields, brushy areas, and wetlands. **RANGE:** Alaska, most of Canada, and south to parts of Midwest and Southeast.

2"

2"

HABITAT: Prairies, plains, and farmlands.
RANGE:

WOLVERINE
Gulo gulo

LOOK FOR: A stocky, fierce-looking, dark brown animal with two wide tan stripes on sides meeting at the tail. **SIZE:** Body 3'–3'6" long. **HABITAT:** Northern forests and tundras. **RANGE:** Alaska, most of Canada, and south to parts of Washington, Oregon, California, Montana, and Colorado.

STRIPED SKUNK
Mephitis mephitis

Skunks are the poison ivy of the animal world. Their spray is so strong it can temporarily blind you even if you are 10 feet away. If sprayed, do not bother washing your clothes—just throw them away. The skunk's bold black-and-white pattern warns other animals to keep away. Any animal that has been sprayed will never forget those distinctive colors.

WESTERN SPOTTED SKUNK
Spilogale gracilis

LOOK FOR: A small skunk with a pattern of black-and-white stripes and white spots on top of its head. **SIZE:** Body 9–12" long.
HABITAT: Woodlands, brushy areas, and farmlands. **RANGE:** Part of southwest Canada and south to most of western U.S.

COMMON HOG-NOSED SKUNK
Conepatus mesoleucus

LOOK FOR: A skunk with white top of body and tail and black lower body and legs. Has a wide nose. **SIZE:** Body 13–20" long.
HABITAT: Brushy areas and foothills. **RANGE:** Colorado, Arizona, Oklahoma, New Mexico, and Texas.

LOOK FOR: A black-and-white furry animal the size of a cat, with a very bushy tail.

SIZE: Body 13–16" long, tail 7–16"; 6–14 lb.

SIGNS: Tracks showing 5 toes. Small holes 3–6" deep dug in the ground. A strong unpleasant odor if skunk has sprayed.

1½"

1¾"

HABITAT: Woodlands, grasslands, deserts, and suburbs.
RANGE:

NORTHERN RIVER OTTER
Lutra canadensis

These intelligent curious animals are best known for their playfulness. Female otters are excellent mothers and teach their babies to swim and catch fish. This may explain why otters are both playful and easily trained.

LOOK FOR: A long, dark brown or black freshwater mammal with a flat-looking head and a long thick furry tail. When swimming, otters will often poke their heads out of the water, puff, snort, hiss, and look around (muskrats and beavers never do this).

SIZE: Body 23–32" long, tail 12–20" long; 11–30 lb.

SEA OTTER
Enhydra lutris

LOOK FOR: A large, dark brown saltwater mammal with a grayish face, short thick tail, and hind feet like flippers. **SIZE:** Body 24–60" long. **HABITAT:** Shallow ocean waters near shores with seaweed and shellfish. **RANGE:** Along Pacific Coast from Alaska to California.

SIGNS: Toes may not show clearly in tracks. Droppings contain fish scales and crayfish shells.

HABITAT: Waters rich in fish, especially lower sections of streams, rivers, and river mouths. Rarely in polluted waters or areas of high human population.
RANGE:

1½"

1½"

MOUNTAIN LION
Felis concolor

LOOK FOR: A large yellowish-tan cat with a very long black-tipped tail.

SIZE: Body 4–6' long, tail 21–37"; 75–275 lb.

SIGNS: Round tracks with no claws showing. Scrapes (dirt kicked up by hind feet) 6–18" across and 1–2" high, often with droppings containing deer hair. Remains of prey covered with leaves. Scratch marks high on tree trunks.

3¼"

3"

HABITAT: In the West, open forests where Mule Deer are plentiful and people are few. In Florida, remote swamps and thickets (the Everglades).

The Mountain Lion, also called the Puma, the Cougar, the Panther, and the Catamount, feeds mostly on deer. The only two other food items it consistently eats are, surprisingly, porcupines and grass. Today Mountain Lions live mainly in western North America. Some, however, live in the Florida Everglades, where they are called Florida Panthers.

RANGE:

CAUTION: Mountain Lions rarely attack people, but if you do encounter one, back up calmly. Do not turn your back and run.

JAGUAR
Panthera onca

LOOK FOR: A large heavy long-tailed cat with a very large head; tan to yellow with brown spots outlined in black and a white belly. Only North American cat that roars. **SIZE:** Body 4–6' long. **HABITAT:** Dense brushes, forests, and swamps. **RANGE:** Southwestern U.S.; very rare.

OCELOT
Felis pardalis

LOOK FOR: A medium-size cat with a long tail. Tan with brown spots outlined in black. **SIZE:** Body 24–36" long. **HABITAT:** Forests and brushy areas. **RANGE:** Southern U.S. (mainly Texas).

BOBCAT
Lynx rufus

The Bobcat is found only in North America and is the most common wildcat here. This cat feeds mainly on rabbits and hares but it will attack many types of prey. A fearless predator, it not only attacks animals larger than itself, it also takes on skunks and porcupines. Its name comes from its "bobbed," or stubby, tail.

LYNX
Lynx lynx

LOOK FOR: A gray long-legged cat with black ear tufts and a short tail tipped in black. **SIZE:** Body 24–36" long. **HABITAT:** Pine forests. **RANGE:** Alaska, most of Canada, and south to Washington, Oregon, Idaho, Montana, Wyoming, and Colorado.

LOOK FOR:. A short-tailed, spotted, yellowish-brown cat with a white belly. Twice the size of a house cat. Seldom seen, but tracks in snow are easily found in the right habitat.

SIZE: Body 24–48" long, tail 4–7"; 14–29 lb.

SIGNS: Round tracks usually in a straight line; claws do not print. Doglike droppings encircled by scratch marks. Calls sound like domestic cat's but also gives piercing scream.

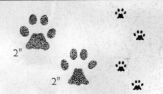

2"

2"

HABITAT: Swamps, forests, farmlands, and brushy areas; rocky ledges preferred for den sites.

RANGE:

COLLARED PECCARY
Tayassu tajacu

LOOK FOR: A small pig with coarse bristly hair in a salt-and-pepper pattern.

SIZE: Body about 3' long, tail 1–2" long; 30–65 lb.

SIGNS: Tracks like small deer tracks. Droppings are loose.

Ground torn up from rooting for food.

1–1½"

1–1½"

HABITAT: Deserts with brushy areas and canyons.

RANGE:

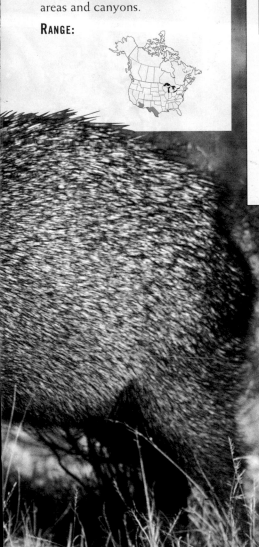

WILD BOAR
Sus scrofas

LOOK FOR: A hairy pig with 3–5" tusks curling up and out of mouth. Hair usually black but may be gray, brown, or black-and-white. **SIZE:** Body 4–5′ long. **HABITAT:** Mountain forests, brushy areas, and swamps. **RANGE:** Throughout southeastern U.S., parts of Northeast and Southwest, California, and Oregon. **CAUTION:** Wild Boars are dangerous; avoid them.

Also known as the Javelina, the Collared Peccary lives in the Southwest where it feeds mainly on prickly pear cacti, grass, seeds, and nuts. It lives in small herds with an equal number of males and females. The Collared Peccary's social behavior is interesting to watch, but do not bother during the heat of the day—high temperatures make these animals inactive.

WHITE-TAILED DEER
Odocoileus virginianus

A century ago, deer were hunted almost to extinction in the East. When conservation laws were passed, deer populations began to grow. Over the century, many acres of farmland and pastures in the East were abandoned and grew into brushland—the perfect deer habitat. Today there are more White-tailed Deer in the United States than when the first settlers landed.

Look for: A deer with a reddish-brown coat in summer or a grayish-brown coat in winter. The big white tail is raised when the deer is bounding away. Bucks have antlers that curve forward.

Size: Body about 6' long, 24–48" high; tail 6–13" long; 90–310 lb.

Signs: Tracks of narrow split hooves. Droppings are hard dark pellets about ¾" long. Body-size areas of flattened grass or snow where deer sleep. Bucks rub antlers on small trees.

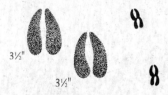

3½"

3½"

Habitat: Suburbs, woods, brushy areas, and farmlands.
Range:

MULE DEER
Odocoileus hemionus

Look for: A deer like the White-tailed but with a larger heavier body, much larger ears, a black-tipped tail, and more upright antlers that branch outward. **Size:** Body 3–7' long. **Habitat:** Forests, sagebrushes, prairies, and mountains. **Range:** Western Canada and U.S. east to Wisconsin and western Texas.

KEY DEER
Odocoileus virginianus clavium

Look for: A tiny dog-size deer similar to the White-tailed Deer found only in the Florida Keys. **Size:** Body about 3' long. **Habitat:** Pine and mangrove forests. **Range:** Florida Keys (mainly Big Pine Key).

ELK
Cervus elaphus

Look for: A very large reddish-brown deer with massive antlers, a light rump patch, and long legs.

Size: Body 6–9' long, about 5' high; tail 3–8" long; 450–1,089 lb.

Signs: Tracks show a cowlike hoof split in two. Winter droppings are like deer pellets, but 1" or larger. Summer droppings are soft, like "cow pies." Antler rubs on small trees. Bulls are very vocal and "bugle" to challenge other males in fall.

Habitat: Western forests. Migrates from mountain meadows in summer, down through several forest types, to sagebrush flats in winter.

Range:

4½"

4½"

The Elk is also called the Wapiti, a Shawnee word meaning "white-rumped deer," referring to the light-colored rump of this impressive deer.

When the first European settlers arrived in North America, the Elk lived in eastern forests and on the prairies, but the eastern Elks were soon hunted to extinction. Today the Elk live mainly in the Rocky Mountains.

CARIBOU
Rangifer tarandus

LOOK FOR: A medium-size deer in various shades of brown with a white throat and neck and massive antlers. Often seen in huge migratory herds; hooves make a clicking sound when Caribou run. Caribou dig deep pits in snow to get at lichens. **SIZE:** Body 4–8' long. **HABITAT:** Tundras and mountainous pine forests. **RANGE:** Throughout Alaska and Canada.

MOOSE
Alces alces

The Moose is the largest deer in the world. The antlers of males, or bulls, may stretch more than 5 feet across and weigh up to 85 pounds. The antlers grow under a layer of living skin called "velvet," which peels off each year. Bulls shed their antlers in winter and begin growing new larger ones in spring.

LOOK FOR: A big cowlike animal, usually dark brown, but colors vary from shades of brown to pale yellow depending on the animal's age and the season. Very long legs for getting through deep snow, big antlers, and a large flap of skin hanging from the neck.

SIZE: Body 6–9' long, 7–8' high; tail about 7" long; 700–1,400 lb.

SIGNS: Tracks show a split hoof like a cow's but more pointed. Droppings are pellets in winter but chips or "pies" in summer when Moose are feeding on freshwater plants. On trails and beds the ground is torn up.

6¼"

6¼"

HABITAT: Northern forests and swamps. Often seen in streamside willow thickets.

RANGE:

PRONGHORN
Antilocapra americana

Although the Pronghorn is easily spotted, it is almost impossible to approach. It can run up to 70 miles an hour, making it the fastest mammal in North America, and its excellent eyesight can detect motion 4 miles away. The Pronghorn is sometimes called the American Antelope.

Look for: A medium-size deerlike animal. Light brown with a white rump and belly.

Size: Body about 4' long, about 3' high; tail 2–7" long; 75–140 lb.

3"

3"

Signs: Deerlike tracks.

Habitat: Grasslands, brushy areas, and agricultural areas.

Range:

AMERICAN BISON
Bos bison

LOOK FOR: A very large, almost black, shaggy cowlike animal with a hump over its shoulders. Both cows and bulls have short curved horns.

SIZE: Body 6–11' long, up to 6' high; tail 12–19" long; 793–2,000 lb.

SIGNS: Tracks and droppings like domestic cow's. Torn up and trampled ground, trees rubbed and dying, large barren dust areas.

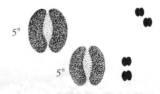

5"

5"

HABITAT: Plains and prairies in the U.S.; and some forested areas in western Canada.

RANGE:

MUSKOX
Ovibos moschatus

LOOK FOR: A bisonlike animal with long shaggy hair and large brown horns that curve downward, close to the head. **SIZE:** Body 6–8' long. **HABITAT:** Arctic tundras. **RANGE:** Canadian Arctic, west of Hudson Bay, and Alaska southeast of Nome.

Once a symbol of the Old West, the American Bison (commonly called the Buffalo) is now used to help restore prairies. Bison help prairies by "rubbing out" trees, treading on seeds with their sharp hooves, and creating plowed ground where new plants can grow.

MOUNTAIN GOAT
Oreamnos americanus

Who would believe that a hoofed animal could live on the icy face of a sheer cliff under frigid winter conditions? Mountain Goats can. Their hooves have hard sharp edges and rubbery soles that help them to get traction on ice and rock. They live on cliffs because no predators can follow them and there is no competition for the grasses and other plants that grow on the hard-to-reach ledges.

LOOK FOR: A long-haired, white, square-looking goat with small black horns and a hump on the shoulders. Easily spotted in summer but nearly invisible when the mountaintops are covered with snow, which is 10 months of the year.

SIZE: Body 4–5' long, 3–4' high; tail 3–8" long; 117–180 lb.

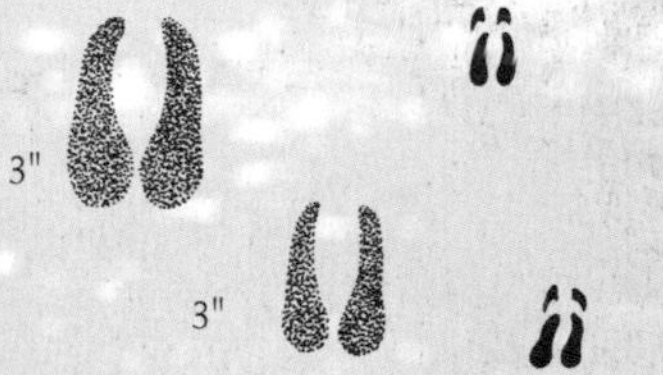

3"

3"

SIGNS: Shed clumps of long white hair on plants and rocks.

HABITAT: Cliffs, tops of ridges, grassy rocky slopes, and alpine meadows.

RANGE:

BIGHORN SHEEP
Ovis canadensis

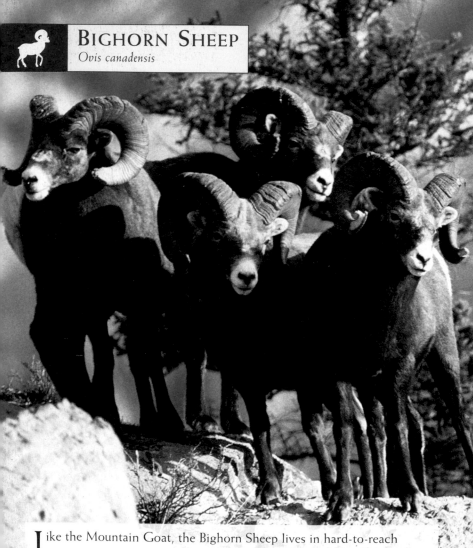

Like the Mountain Goat, the Bighorn Sheep lives in hard-to-reach mountainous areas. But unlike the Mountain Goat, the Bighorn also lives at lower elevations and in warmer, more southern regions, even deserts. At times, these sheep will roam out onto meadows or prairies if cliffs to escape to are nearby.

DALL'S SHEEP
Ovis dalli

LOOK FOR: A pure white version of the Bighorn but with thinner horns. **SIZE:** Body 3–5' long. **HABITAT:** Mountain areas. **RANGE:** Alaska and northwestern Canada.

LOOK FOR: A brown sheep with a white snout, rump, and belly. Massive horns in a tight spiral. Can be seen in small herds of 5 to 15.

SIZE: Body 4–6' long, 3–4' high; tail 4–6" long; 74–316 lb.

SIGNS: Tracks like a deer's. Dark bell-shaped droppings.

HABITAT: Rocky cliffs and canyons from alpine tundras to deserts.

RANGE:

3½"

3½"

HARBOR SEAL
Phoca vitulina

This well-named seal is the most common seal you will see along the Atlantic coast. They live near shore and spend much of the day basking on small islands. They are large, bigger than a large man, and are usually a spotted gray, tan, or dark brown. Their populations have increased considerably in recent years, and they are not popular with fishermen because they eat mostly fish. Like all seals they are sometimes eaten by sharks.

LOOK FOR: A small seal often seen lying on rocks. It comes in many colors and patterns but is usually light gray to brown with spots.

SIZE: Body 4–6' long, tail 3–5" long; up to 308 lb.

SIGNS: Sometimes located by their barking.

HABITAT: Waters near shore, especially river mouths and harbors.

RANGE:

GRAY SEAL
Halichoerus grypus

LOOK FOR: A large gray to black seal with a long snout. Barks; also makes quavering calls. **SIZE:** Body 8–10' long. **HABITAT:** Waters near shore with rocky coasts and islands. **RANGE:** Labrador south to New England.

NORTHERN ELEPHANT SEAL
Mirounga angustirostris

LOOK FOR: A very large, brown or gray seal. Males have a large inflatable nose that can hang limply, somewhat like an elephant's trunk. **SIZE:** Body 10–13' long. **HABITAT:** Spends most of its time in mild seas. **RANGE:** In Pacific waters from Alaska to southern California.

139

CALIFORNIA SEA LION
Zalophus californianus

This is the beloved trained seal of the circus. The California Sea Lion is very fast, playful, and able to catch things in the air with its teeth. It is as playful in the wild as it is when tamed, riding the surf, and leaping in and out of the water. Often seen basking on land by day, the sea lion feeds at night. It can dive as deep as 450 feet below the surface of the water.

LOOK FOR: A brown seal with a tan face; females are lighter in color than males.

SIZE: Body 5–8' long; 100–860 lb.

SIGNS: Barks, wails, and bleats.

HABITAT: Island beaches or rocky coasts.

RANGE:

NORTHERN SEA LION
Eumetopias jubatus

LOOK FOR: A large, light brown to black seal with coarse hair and a massive neck. **SIZE:** Body 6–11' long. **HABITAT:** Near shore along rocky coastlines. **RANGE:** Southern Alaska and south to southern California.

NORTHERN FUR SEAL
Callorhinus ursinus

LOOK FOR: A dark brown seal with very large flippers and a tiny tail. Males have an enlarged neck. Makes loud coughs, barks, and bleating calls. **SIZE:** Body 4–7' long. **HABITAT:** Open seas except for summer breeding on islands. **RANGE:** Alaska south to California.

141

The West Indian Manatee is an endangered species. For many years it was killed for meat. Now its habitat in the coastal waters of Florida is heavily used by people for boating and is being disturbed by development. Saving the manatee will be difficult. It does not breed in captivity, and its population continues to decline

LOOK FOR: A very large, torpedo shaped aquatic mammal with a paddle-shaped tail and front flippers. Moves at a moderate speed through the water.

SIZE: Body 10–13' long; 1,100–3,500 lb.

SIGNS: Two nostrils above the surface of the water.

HABITAT: Tropical and subtropical waters near shore where sea grass or freshwater vegetation grows.

RANGE:

HUMPBACK WHALE
Megaptera novaeangliae

This whale is the favorite of whale watchers because its tail and back come out of the water as it swims and dives. They also "breach" (jump clear of the water) and sometimes wave their front flippers in the air. They are quite common in both the Atlantic and Pacific oceans and have beautiful, haunting songs.

LOOK FOR: A large whale with very long white flippers. Body is black on top, white on the bottom. Usually covered with barnacles, bumps, and knobs, especially on the head.

SIZE: Body up to 50' long; up to 60,000 lb.

SIGNS: A single spout shooting straight up for 10'.

HABITAT: Deep coastal waters.

RANGE:

NORTHERN RIGHT WHALE
Balaena glacialis

LOOK FOR: A large spotted brown whale with no fin on back. Has a very large mouth with brushlike teeth for filtering plankton. Has a V-shaped double spout that angles forward up to 16' high. **SIZE:** Body up to 60' long. **HABITAT:** Shallow bays and nearshore waters. **RANGE:** Northern seas south to Florida and California.

GRAY WHALE
Eschrichtius robustus

LOOK FOR: A large brownish-gray whale covered with white blotches, spots, scars, and barnacles. No fin on back. Spout shoots up in a V shape. **SIZE:** Body up to 46' long. **HABITAT:** Shallow bays, inlets, and nearshore waters. **RANGE:** Pacific coastline from Canada to Mexico. Commonly seen along the California coast. Atlantic population was hunted to extinction.

145

KILLER WHALE
Orcinus orca

These highly intelligent, social whales have developed ways of hunting in groups that are similar to the hunting methods of wolves and lions. They are fearsome predators that can kill a wide range of animals, such as Blue Whales, seals, sea turtles, squid, and fish. Fortunately, they do not seem to have a taste for people; there are no records of humans attacked by Killer Whales.

LOOK FOR: A medium-size, boldly marked, black-and-white whale with a high straight dorsal fin.

SIZE: Body up to 32' long; up to 18,000 lb.

SIGNS: High straight fin on back (3–6' long) can be seen from a

SPERM WHALE
Physeter catodon

LOOK FOR: A large, dark brownish-gray whale with a "hump" on its back followed by little bumps down to the broad notched tail. Big squarish snout angles forward. **SIZE:** Body up to 69' long. **HABITAT:** Tropical and temperate seas in waters 600–10,000' deep. **RANGE:** In Atlantic and Pacific oceans, from northern Canada south to northern South America.

SHORT-FINNED PILOT WHALE
Globiocephala macrorhynchus

LOOK FOR: A medium-size black whale with a gray belly. Usually seen in large herds. **SIZE:** Body up to 23' long. **HABITAT:** Tropical and temperate waters. **RANGE:** In Pacific Ocean from Alaska south to Guatemala. In Atlantic Ocean from New Jersey south to Venezuela.

distance. Sometimes pokes its head above water, breaches, or jumps.

HABITAT: Deep coastal waters.

RANGE:

147

BOTTLENOSED DOLPHIN
Tursiops truncatus

Bottlenosed Dolphins are highly intelligent and curious mammals that are often used in aquarium shows. These dolphins follow fishing boats to feed on the fish that are thrown back; they have even been known to approach swimmers. Like bats, they locate prey using echolocation.

Porpoises, though similar to dolphins, are much smaller and are seen less often in North American waters.

LOOK FOR: A friendly dolphin with a wide back fin. Dark gray back, light gray on the sides.

SIZE: Body up to 12' long; up to 1,400 lb.

SIGNS: Back fin rhythmically

COMMON DOLPHIN
Delphinus delphis

LOOK FOR: A slender brownish-black dolphin with a white belly. Dark stripe from jaw to flipper. **SIZE:** Body up to 9' long. **HABITAT:** Waters offshore. **RANGE:** In Atlantic and Pacific oceans from Canada south to northern South America.

PACIFIC WHITE-SIDED DOLPHIN
Lagenorhynchus obliquidens

LOOK FOR: A dolphin with a curved back. Has a black-and-white belly. Rides the bow waves of ships. **SIZE:** Body up to 8' long. **HABITAT:** Coastal waters to 100 miles out to sea. **RANGE:** Alaska to southern California.

breaks the water. Rides the bow waves of ships.

HABITAT: Shallow nearshore waters, bays, and river mouths.

RANGE:

Pronghorn page 130

How to use the reference section

The **Glossary,** which begins below, contains terms used by mammalogists and naturalists. If you run across a word in this book that you do not understand, check the glossary for a definition. Also in this section is a listing of **Resources**, including books, videotapes, CDs, Web sites, and organizations devoted to North American mammals, as well as a table for learning how to convert measurements to metrics. Finally, there is an **Index** of all the species covered in the Field Guide section of this book.

GLOSSARY

Aggressive
Describes an animal that is bold or that starts fights easily.

Aquatic
Found in water.

Bound
To leap.

Breach
To jump out of the water.

Burrow
A hole or tunnel dug in the ground for shelter.

Carnivore
An animal that eats meat.

Den
A safe hidden place, often an animal's home; may be in a hole in a tree or log, a tunnel under the ground, or under a rock or a bush.

Echolocation
A method used by bats and dolphins for "seeing" objects or prey. A bat, for example, makes high-pitched squeaking sounds while flying. The sounds bounce off objects and back to the bat's ears; from the returning sounds the animal understands where objects or prey lie.

Forelimb
The front leg or front flipper.

Fungi
Mushrooms, molds, mildews, and yeasts.

Habitat
The environment in which an animal lives.

Hibernation
A long deep sleep, usually over the winter, when an animal's heartbeat and breathing slow way down and its body temperature drops.

Hind limb
The back leg or back flipper.

Home range
The area of a mammal's habitat that it lives in and wanders around in day to day.

Invertebrates
Animals without spinal columns, or backbones, such as insects and earthworms.

Lichen
A plant made up of algae and fungi; often grows on rocks.

Litter
The babies born at a single birth.

Lodge
A den, usually the stick home a beaver builds on a pond or in a stream.

Migrate
To move from one place to another, usually for feeding, breeding, or giving birth; mammals usually migrate at the same times and to the same places year after year.

New World
North and South America.

Nocturnal
Active at night.

Predator
An animal that hunts and kills other animals for food.

Prey
An animal caught by predators for food.

Quills
The needlelike spines that cover porcupines.

Rabies
A deadly disease that humans can get from the bite of an animal; in North America, raccoons are the most common carriers. An animal that has rabies is called rabid.

Range
The geographic area where a species normally lives.

Rodents
A group of mostly small mammals with four front teeth that are made for gnawing; chipmunks, squirrels, woodchucks, rats, mice, voles, beavers, muskrats, and porcupines are all rodents.

Roost
A place where flying animals, like birds and bats, come to rest. To roost means to come to the resting place.

Rump
An animal's rear end.

Scat
An animal's droppings.

Solitary
Describes an animal that usually lives alone, not in a group.

Species
Animals that look alike and can mate and have babies with each other.

Walruses

RESOURCES

FOR FURTHER READING

Dangerous Mammals of North America
(Encyclopedia of Danger Series)
Missy Allen and Michel Peissel
Chelsea House Publishers, 1993

Endangered Mammals!
(Endangered Series)
Bob Burton
Gareth Stevens, Inc., 1996

Endangered Ocean Animals
(Endangered Animals Series)
J. David Taylor
Crabtree Publishing Co., 1992

Extremely Weird Mammals
Sarah Lovett
John Muir Publications, 1996

Forest Mammals
(North American Wildlife Series)
Bobbie Kalman
Crabtree Publishing Co., 1987

Grassland Mammals
(True Book Series)
Elaine Landau
Children's Press, 1997

Large Mammals Activity Book
Parkwest Publications, 1993

Mammal
(Eyewitness Books Series)
Steve Parker
Alfred A. Knopf, 1989

Mammals
(Eyewitness Explorers Series)
David Burnie and Jennifer Burnie
Dorling-Kindersley, 1993

Mind-Blowing Mammals
(Amazing Animals Series)
Leslee Elliott
Sterling Publications, 1995

National Audubon Society Book of Wild Animals
Les Line and Edward R. Ricciuti (Eds.)
Wings Books, 1996

National Audubon Society Field Guide to North American Mammals
John O. Whitaker, Jr.
Alfred A. Knopf, revised 1996

National Audubon Society Pocket Guide to Familiar Animal Tracks of North America
John Farrand, Jr.
Alfred A. Knopf, 1993

National Audubon Society Pocket Guide to Familiar Mammals of North America
John Farrand, Jr.
Alfred A. Knopf, 1988

National Audubon Society Pocket Guide to Familiar Marine Mammals of North America
Stephen H. Amos
Alfred A. Knopf, 1990

Saving Endangered Mammals: A Field Guide to Some of the Earth's Rarest Animals
(Cincinnati Zoo Book)
Thane Maynard
Franklin Watts, Inc., 1992

Sea Mammals
(Pointers Series)
Anita Ganeri
Steck-Vaughn Co., 1996

Small Mammals
(Nature Detective Series)
Anita Ganeri
Franklin Watts, Inc., 1993

Watching Wildlife: Tips, Gear, and Great Places for Enjoying America's Wild Creatures
Mark Damian Duda
Falcon Press Publishing, 1995

What Is a Mammal?
Robert Snedden
Sierra Club, 1994

Wildlife Viewing Guides
(Watchable Wildlife Series)
Falcon Press Publishing

TAPES AND DISKS

All American Bear
(Nova Video Library, Adventures in Science)
Vestron Video, 1988

The Grizzlies
(National Geographic Videos)
Vestron Video, 1987

In the Company of Whales
(Interactive CD-ROM)
Discovery Communications, Inc., 1993

Polar Bear Alert
(National Geographic Videos)
Vestron Video, 1982

Rocky Mountain Beaver Pond
(National Geographic Videos)
Columbia Tristar Home Video, 1987

Whale Watch
(Nova Video Library, Adventures in Science)
Vestron Video, 1982

White Wolf
(National Geographic Videos)
Columbia Tristar Home Video, 1988

ORGANIZATIONS

EarthWatch International
680 Mount Auburn Street
P.O. Box 403
Watertown, MA 02272
Tel: 800-776-0188
http://www.earthwatch.org

Defenders of Wildlife
1101 14th Street NW, #1400
Washington, DC 20005
Tel: 202-682-9400
http://www.defenders.org

National Audubon Society
700 Broadway
New York, NY 10003-9562
Tel: 800-274-4201
http://www.audubon.org

National Wildlife Federation
8925 Leesburg Pike
Vienna, VA 22184
Tel: 703-790-4100
http://www.nwf.org/nwf/
home.html

The Nature Conservancy
International Headquarters
1815 North Lynn Street
Arlington, VA 22209
Tel: 703-841-5300
http://www.tnc.org

Sierra Club
85 2nd Street, 2nd Floor
San Francisco, CA 94105-3441
Tel: 415-977-5500
http://www.sierraclub.org

WEB SITES

Audubon Web Site for Kids:
http://www.audubon.org/kid/
index.html

The Electronic Zoo:
http://netvet.wustl.edu/e-zoo.htm

National Wildlife Federation's Kid's Page:
http://www.nwf.org/kids

Smithsonian Institution, Mammal Species of the World:
http://www.nmnh.si.edu/msw

Wolf's Den Web Site:
http://www.wolfsden.org

West Indian Manatee page 142

Make it metric

Here is a chart you can use to change measurements of size, distance, weight, and temperature to their metric equivalents.

	multiply by
inches to millimeters	25
inches to centimeters	2.5
feet to meters	0.3
yards to meters	0.9
miles to kilometers	1.6
square miles to square kilometers	2.6
ounces to grams	28.3
pounds to kilograms	.45
Fahrenheit to Centigrade	subtract 32 and multiply by .55

INDEX

Page numbers in **bold type** point to a mammal's page in the field guide.

Grizzly Bear page 105

Lynx page 121

Mountain Pocket Gopher

Kit Fox   page 103

PHOTO/ILLUSTRATION CREDITS

47e: Stephen J. Krasemann/Photo Researchers
48: Rod Planck
50–51: Joe McDonald
52–53: Rod Planck
53a: Rob & Ann Simpson
53b: B. Moose Peterson/WRP
54–55:Gerry Ellis/Ellis Nature Photography
54 (inset): Rob & Ann Simpson
55a: Rob Curtis/The Early Birder
55b: Gary Meszaros/Dembinsky Photo Assoc.
56–57: Joe McDonald
57a: James F. Parnell
57b: James F. Parnell
58 59: Stephen Dalton/Photo Researchers
58 (inset): Merlin D. Tuttle/Bruce Coleman, Inc.
59a: Merlin D. Tuttle/Bruce Coleman, Inc.
59b: Merlin D. Tuttle/Bruce Coleman, Inc.
60–61: Daniel J. Cox/Natural Exposures, Inc.
62–63: Pat & Tom Leeson/Photo Researchers
63: Harry M. Walker
64–65: Rod Planck
65a: Anthony Mercieca/Root Resources
65b: Stan Osolinski
66–67: Harry M. Walker
67 (inset): Rod Planck
67: Francisco Erize/Bruce Coleman, Inc.
68–69: Maslowski Photo
69a: G.C. Kelley
69b: G.C. Kelley/Photo Researchers
70–71: Steve Maslowski/Photo Researchers
71a: Robert Pollock
71b: Tom J. Ulrich
72–73: Chuck Gordon
73a: Eric & David Hosking/Photo Researchers
73b: Rod Planck
74–75: Mark F. Wallner
75a: G.C. Kelley
75b: Charlie Ott/Photo Researchers
76–77: Rod Planck/Photo Researchers
77a: John Cancalosi
77b: B. Moose Peterson/WRP
78–79: Rod Planck
79a: Sharon Cummings
79b: Michael H. Francis
79c: Nick Bergkessel/Photo Researchers
80–81: Tom McHugh/Photo Researchers
81a: Jeff Foott
81b: William P. Leonard
82–83: Joe McDonald

83a: Joe McDonald
83b: Roger Barbour/Photo Researchers
83c: Rob & Ann Simpson
84–85: Tom McHugh/Photo Researchers
85a: B. Moose Peterson/WRP
85b: Alvin E. Staffan/Photo Researchers
85c: R.J. Erwin/Photo Researchers
86–87: Dale & Marian Zimmerman
87a: Ronn Altig
87b: Jeff Foott
87c: C. Allan Morgan
88–89: Tom McHugh/Photo Researchers
89a: Betty Randall
89b: Ron Austing
89c: James F. Parnell
90–91: Rob & Ann Simpson
91a: Rob & Ann Simpson
91b: Karl H. Maslowski/Photo Researchers
92–93: Mark F. Wallner
94–95: Tom J. Ulrich
95: Rob Curtis/The Early Birder
96–97: Rita Summers
98–99: Rod Planck
100–101: Jeff Lepore/Photo Researchers
101: James H. Robinson
102–103: Tom & Pat Leeson/Photo Researchers
103a: Daniel J. Cox/Natural Exposures, Inc.
103b: Larry Sansone
103c: Rita Summers
104–105: Pat & Tom Leeson/Photo Researchers
105a: Pat & Tom Leeson/Photo Researchers
105b: Stan Osolinski
106–107: Joe McDonald
107a: Kevin Schafer
107b: G.C. Kelley
108–109: Michael H. Francis
109a: Tom J. Ulrich
109b: Michael H. Francis
110–111: Charles G. Summers, Jr.
111a: Betty Randall
111b: Jeff Vanuga
111c: James F. Parnell
112–113: Karen McClymonds
113: Karen McClymonds
114–115: Jeff Foott
115a: Anthony Mercieca/Root Resources
115b: Perry Shankle, Jr.
116–117: Richard Day/Daybreak Imagery
117: J. Eastcott & Y. Momatiuk/Photo Researchers
118–119: Charles G. Summers, Jr.
119a: Renee Lynn/Photo Researchers
119b: C. Allan Morgan
120–121: Jeff Lepore/Photo Researchers

121: Richard Day/Daybreak Imagery
122–123: G.C. Kelley
123: Leonard Lee Rue, Jr.
124–125: Leonard Lee Rue III/Photo Researchers
125a: Michael H. Francis
125b: James H. Robinson
126–127: Phil A. Dotson/Photo Researchers
127: Harry M. Walker
128 129: Harry M. Walker
130–131: Michael Durham/Ellis Nature Photography
132–133: Gerald & Buff Corsi/Focus on Nature, Inc.
133: Dominique Braud/Dembinsky Photo Assoc.
134–135: B. Moose Peterson/WRP
136–137: Michael H. Francis
137: Michael H. Francis
138–139: Karen McClymonds
139a: Tom McHugh/Photo Researchers
139b: C. Allan Morgan
140–141: Julin D. Hyde/Wild Things Photography
141a: Tom & Pat Leeson/Photo Researchers
141b: Tom J. Ulrich
142–143: Douglas Faulkner/Photo Researchers
144–145: John B. Hyde/Wild Things Photography
145a: James D. Watt/Waterhouse Stock Photography
145b: Kevin Schafer
146–147: Doug Perrine/Innerspace Visions
147a: François Gohier/Photo Researchers
147b: James D. Watt/Innerspace Visions
148–149: James D. Watt/Waterhouse Stock Photography
149a: François Gohier/Photo Researchers
149b: Jeff Pantukhoff/Innerspace Visions
150: Rod Planck
151: Rod Planck
153: Douglas Faulkner/Photo Researchers
154: Rod Planck
155: Daniel J. Cox/Natural Exposures, Inc.
156: Richard R. Hansen/Photo Researchers
157: Stephen J. Krasemann/Photo Researchers

*Photo Researchers, Inc.
60 East 56th Street
New York, NY 10022

Prepared and produced by
Chanticleer Press, Inc.

Publisher: Andrew Stewart
Founder: Paul Steiner

Chanticleer Staff:
Editor-in-Chief: Amy K. Hughes
Editor: Miriam Harris
Assistant Editor: Michelle Bredeson
Editorial Assistants: Kate Jacobs, Tessa Kale
Photo Director: Zan Carter
Photo Traffic Coordinator: Jennifer McClanaghan
Rights and Permissions Manager: Alyssa Sachar
Art Director: Drew Stevens
Designer: Vincent Mejia
Assistant Designer: Anthony Liptak
Director of Production: Alicia Mills
Production Assistant: Philip Pfeifer
Publishing Assistant: Karin Murphy

Contributors:
Writer (The world of mammals, How to look at mammals): John Grassy
Writer (The field guide): Chuck Keene
Mammal Tracks: Howard S. Friedman
Icons: Holly Kowitt

Scholastic, Inc., Staff:
Editorial Director: Wendy Barish, Creative Director: David Saylor,
Managing Editor: Manuela Soares, Manufacturing Manager: Janet Castiglione

Original Series Design: Chic Simple Design